Patrick Suppes, Economics, and Economic Methodology

Patrick Suppes (1922–2014) was an extraordinarily wide-ranging scholar. Although best known as a philosopher of science, Suppes made substantial contributions to a remarkably wide range of different fields of research including many relevant to economics: decision theory, philosophy of economics, modeling theory, foundations of measurement, philosophy of psychology (and thus what is now behavioral economics), and many other fields. This collection recognizes Suppes's contributions to economics and economic methodology with a symposium of papers that examine, build on, and/or assess Suppes's research in these areas. The authors include philosophers, economists, game theorists, historians of economics, and many whose research combine these fields. This book honors Patrick Suppes, while at the same time, exhibiting the richness of contemporary philosophy of economics.

It was originally published as a special issue of the *Journal of Economic Methodology*.

John B. Davis is Professor of Economics at Marquette University, USA, and Professor of Economics at the University of Amsterdam, the Netherlands. He is the author of *Keynes's Philosophical Development* (1994), *The Theory of the Individual in Economics: Identity and Value* (2003), and *Individuals and Identity in Economics* (2011), and co-author of *Economic Methodology: Understanding Economics as a Science* (2011, with Marcel Boumans). He is co-editor of the *Journal of Economic Methodology* and *The Elgar Companion to Recent Economic Methodology* (2011, with D. Wade Hands).

D. Wade Hands is Distinguished Professor of Economics at the University of Puget Sound, USA. He is the author of *Testing, Rationality, and Progress: Essays on the Popperian Tradition in Economic Methodology* (1993), *Reflection Without Rules: Economic Methodology and Contemporary Science Theory* (2001), *Introductory Mathematical Economics*, 2nd edition (2004), and co-author of *Agreement on Demand: Consumer Theory in the Twentieth Century* (2006, with Philip Mirowski). He is co-editor of the *Journal of Economic Methodology* and *The Elgar Companion to Recent Economic Methodology* (2011, with John B. Davis).

Patrick Suppes, Economics, and Economic Methodology

Edited by
John B. Davis and D. Wade Hands

Routledge
Taylor & Francis Group

LONDON AND NEW YORK

First published 2018 by Routledge

2 Park Square, Milton Park, Abingdon, Oxfordshire OX14 4RN
52 Vanderbilt Avenue, New York, NY 10017

Routledge is an imprint of the Taylor & Francis Group, an informa business

First issued in paperback 2019

British Library Cataloguing in Publication Data
A catalogue record for this book is available from the British Library

ISBN 13: 978-1-138-50407-3 (hbk)
ISBN 13: 978-0-367-89184-8 (pbk)

Typeset in TimesNewRomanPS
by diacriTech, Chennai

Publisher's Note
The publisher accepts responsibility for any inconsistencies that may have arisen
during the conversion of this book from journal articles to book chapters, namely
the possible inclusion of journal terminology.

Disclaimer
Every effort has been made to contact copyright holders for their permission to
reprint material in this book. The publishers would be grateful to hear from any
copyright holder who is not here acknowledged and will undertake to rectify any
errors or omissions in future editions of this book.

Contents

Citation Information

The chapters in this book were originally published in the *Journal of Economic Methodology*, volume 23, issue 3 (September 2016). When citing this material, please use the original page numbering for each article, as follows:

Chapter 7
Freedom and choice in economics
Adolfo García de la Sienra
Journal of Economic Methodology, volume 23, issue 3 (September 2016) pp. 316–332

Chapter 8
The world in axioms: an interview with Patrick Suppes
Catherine Herfeld
Journal of Economic Methodology, volume 23, issue 3 (September 2016) pp. 333–346

For any permission-related enquiries please visit:
http://www.tandfonline.com/page/help/permissions

Notes on Contributors

Jean Baccelli is a Postdoctoral Researcher at the Munich Center for Mathematical Philosophy, Germany. His research interests lie mainly in the philosophy of economics. His research focuses especially on individual decision theory.

Ken Binmore is Emeritus Professor of Economics at University College London, UK. He has contributed to game theory, experimental economics, evolutionary biology, and moral philosophy. He currently works in decision theory. His books include *Natural Justice, Does Game Theory Work?*, *Game Theory: A Very Short Introduction*, and *Rational Decisions*.

Marcel Boumans is an Associate Professor at the Utrecht University, the Netherlands. His main research focus is on understanding empirical research practices outside the laboratory, from a philosophy of science-in-practice perspective. He is particularly interested in the practices of measurement and modeling and the role of mathematics in social science.

John B. Davis is Professor of Economics at Marquette University, USA, and Professor of Economics at the University of Amsterdam, the Netherlands. He is the author of *Keynes's Philosophical Development* (1994), *The Theory of the Individual in Economics: Identity and Value* (2003), and *Individuals and Identity in Economics* (2011), and co-author of *Economic Methodology: Understanding Economics as a Science* (2011, with Marcel Boumans). He is co-editor of the *Journal of Economic Methodology* and *The Elgar Companion to Recent Economic Methodology* (2011, with D. Wade Hands).

Adolfo García de la Sienra is a Research Professor at the Instituto de Filosofía of Universidad Veracruzana, Mexico. He is the author of *The Logical Foundations of the Marxian Theory of Value* (1992) and several papers on topics within the field of the philosophy of economics. His main fields of interest are the philosophy of economics, philosophy of religion, and general philosophy.

D. Wade Hands is Distinguished Professor of Economics at the University of Puget Sound, USA. He is the author of *Testing, Rationality, and Progress: Essays on the Popperian Tradition in Economic Methodology* (1993), *Reflection Without Rules: Economic Methodology and Contemporary Science Theory* (2001), *Introductory Mathematical Economics*, 2nd edition (2004), and co-author of *Agreement on Demand: Consumer Theory in the Twentieth Century* (2006, with Philip Mirowski). He is co-editor of the *Journal of Economic Methodology* and *The Elgar Companion to Recent Economic Methodology* (2011, with John B. Davis).

NOTES ON CONTRIBUTORS

Catherine Herfeld is an Assistant Professor of Social Theory and Philosophy of the Social Sciences at the University of Zurich, Switzerland. She is also affiliated with the Munich Center for Mathematical Philosophy at Ludwig-Maximilian University (LMU) of Munich, Germany.

Philippe Mongin is Director of Research at Centre National de la Recherche Scientifique and Professor at the HEC Paris, France. He has contributed several books and more than 100 articles on normative economics, individual and collective decision theory, philosophical logic, and the philosophy of economics and the social sciences. His current work is mostly in the latter field.

Ivan Moscati is an Associate Professor of Economics at Insubria University, Varese, Italy, and teaches History of Economics at Bocconi University, Milan, Italy. His research focuses on the history and methodology of microeconomics, with special attention to choice and utility theory. He is an associate editor of the *Journal of Economic Methodology* and the *Journal of the History of Economic Thought*.

Julian Reiss is a Professor of Philosophy at Durham University, UK, and co-director of the Centre for Humanities Engaging Science and Society (CHESS), UK. He is the author of *Error in Economics: Towards a More Evidence-Based Methodology* (2008), *Philosophy of Economics: A Contemporary Introduction* (2013), *Causation, Evidence, and Inference* (2015), and over 50 journal articles and book chapters on topics in the philosophy of the biomedical, social, and economic sciences.

Introduction to symposium on 'Patrick Suppes, economics, and economic methodology'

D. Wade Hands

Patrick Suppes (1922–2014) was an extraordinarily wide-ranging scholar. Although best known as a philosopher of science, Suppes made substantial contributions to a remarkably wide range of different fields of research. In his 'self-profile' published in 1979, Suppes himself organized his research under seven headings: 'foundations of physics; theory of measurement; decision theory; foundations of probability and causality; foundations of psychology; philosophy of language; education and computers; and philosophy and science' (Suppes, 1979, p. 9). Although there is no explicit mention of economics in this list of fields, a number of these different research areas intersect with important fields of economic research. It is also important to note that although much of Suppes' economics-relevant research was produced early in his career, and even though some of this early research was not considered economics at the time; the growth of fields like experimental economics, behavioral economics, and evidence-based economics, clearly makes it relevant to economics and economic methodology today.

Two of many examples of his early research with direct relevance to economics are his two books (Davidson, Suppes, & Siegel, 1957; Suppes & Atkinson, 1960). The former was an experimental study designed to test a version of expected utility theory (work which would now be considered experimental and/or behavioral economics) and the latter was a game-theory-based study of stochastic learning which he later applied to duopoly theory (Suppes & Carlsmith, 1962) and which suggested a new theory of consumer demand (Garcia de la Sienra, 2011). In addition to such specific examples, Suppes made substantive contributions to a number of broader areas of inquiry with relevance to economics and economic methodology: for example decision theory (theoretical, empirical, and normative), measurement theory (an on-going research project essentially throughout his professional life), probabilistic causality (a topic of continued interest in econometric methodology), and the set-theoretic axiomatization of scientific theories (consistent with much of economic theorizing during the 1950s and 1960s – in Arrow-Debreu general equilibrium theory and social choice theory in particular – but also relevant to the philosophy of economics during the 1980s in works like Stegmüller, Balzer, & Spohn, 1982).

One area of Suppes' philosophical research that has become increasingly important to scholars working in economic methodology and the philosophy of economics is his work on scientific models. In the 1960s when most philosophers of science focused exclusively on scientific theories, Suppes (1960, 1962, 1967) began a research program on the nature and character of scientific models that continued throughout his life. Models have been receiving increased attention within general philosophy of science (e.g. Giere, 1999; Weisberg, 2013) and Suppes' work has played an important role in this change:

> The shifting of the attention from language to models is one of the most original features in Suppes' account of scientific theories. Suppes is probably the first philosopher to assign the concept of model a key role in the philosophy of science. In the picture of scientific theory seen as a calculus with correspondence rules, no space is left for introducing models as a way of characterizing theories. (Ferrario & Schiaffonati, 2012, p. 70)

But given the model-building character of economics (Morgan, 2012), scientific models and Suppes' characterization of scientific models are particularly important in the philosophy of economics. The philosophical literature on economic models has expanded rapidly in recent years – a small, but important, sample includes Mäki (2013), Morgan and Knuuttila (2012), Sugden (2000), and the eight papers in the *Erkenntnis* special issue on economic modeling Grüne-Yanoff (2009) – and this literature often makes reference to various ideas in Suppes' work.

One specific example is Suppes' discussion of the 'hierarchy of models' (Suppes, 1960, 1962, 1967) which replaces the logical empiricist correspondence rules connecting scientific theories to empirical data with a hierarchy of different types of models:

> One of the besetting sins of philosophers of science is to overly simplify the structure of science. Philosophers who write about the representation of scientific theories as logical calculi then go on to say that a theory is given empirical meaning by providing interpretations or coordinating definitions for some of the primitive or defined terms of the calculus. What I have attempted to argue is that a whole hierarchy of models stands between the model of the basic theory and the complete experimental experience. Moreover, for each level of the hierarchy there is a theory in its own right. Theory at one level is given empirical meaning by making formal connections with theory at a lower level. (Suppes, 1962, p. 260)

Suppes' hierarchy of models seems to be particularly relevant to the relationship between theory and evidence in economics and has played an important role in the recent literature on economic models (see for example, the Boumans paper in this symposium).

Given all this, the editors of *The Journal of Economic Methodology* wanted to recognize Suppes's contributions to economics and economic methodology with a symposium of papers that examine, build on, or assess Suppes's research in these areas. The papers in the symposium cover an extremely wide range of topics. In 'Patrick Suppes and Game Theory,' Ken Binmore examines two of the ways in which Suppes made substantive contributions to areas of game theory that were relatively out of favor at the time of his contributions. The first was his experimental work (Suppes & Atkinson, 1960) on minimax strategies in zero sum games and the second was his early work (Suppes, 1966) on empathetic preferences which influenced later research on interpersonal utility comparisons by Harsanyi (1977), Binmore (2005), and others. Ivan Moscati's paper 'Measurement Theory and Utility Analysis in Suppes' Early Work: 1951–1958' argues that Suppes' early work on utility theory in association with the Stanford Value Theory Project (Davidson, McKinsey, & Suppes, 1955; Suppes & Winet, 1955; and other research) prompted his change from a classical approach to measurement theory to a representational view of measurement in his later work.

The paper thus demonstrates the rich cross-fertilization of Suppes' research in the economics-relevant areas of decision and measurement theory. The contribution by Jean Baccelli and Philippe Mongin, 'Choice-Based Cardinal Utility: a Tribute to Patrick Suppes,' traces the history of utility theory and distinguishes several different versions of cardinal utility theory. They examine one of these – choice-based cardinalism – in detail and trace it to Suppes' research: Davidson et al. (1957) and related literature on the empirical side and Suppes and Winet (1955) on the concept of utility differences. In 'Suppes' Probabilistic Theory of Causality and Causal Inference in Economics,' Julian Reiss examines Suppes' *Probabilistic Theory of Causality* (1970) from the perspective of causal inference in economics. In the process of this examination he discusses Bayesian networks, evidence (or design) based econometrics, and statistical minimalism, as well as traditional structural approaches. Marcel Boumans' 'Suppes's Outlines of an Empirical Measurement Theory' examines the difference between the way that Suppes characterized the relationship between theory and evidence in scientific theories in general and within his theory of measurement (particularly in Suppes and Zinnes [1963] and the three *Foundations of Measurement* volumes of Krantz, Luce, Suppes, and Tversky [1971/1989/1990]). Boumans proposes a measurement account that applies Suppes' more liberal hierarchy of models characterization of the relationship between theory and practice. In 'Freedom and Choice in Economics,' Adolfo García de la Sienra examines the evolution of Suppes' approach to utility theory and the associated concepts of choice, freedom, and rationality. He argues that Suppes' final position (particularly in Suppes, 1984, 1996, 2001) was a stochastic conception of choice that was relatively critical of rational choice theory. The symposium closes with Catherine Herfeld's interview with Suppes conducted in March 2014 where he provided a detailed discussion of his research and the way that his views evolved over time. The various topics discussed in the interview range widely, and touch repeatedly on the issues of measurement, probability, axiomatization, and decision theory, that are so important to Suppes' view of economics and economic methodology.

All in all it is an excellent set of papers that honors Suppes' lifetime of work, but they also show how his ideas are still alive and relevant to current methodological debates in various areas of economics. The editors hope that these papers spark additional research into the contact points between Suppes' work and economic science.

Disclosure statement

No potential conflict of interest was reported by the author.

References

Binmore, K. (2005). *Natural justice*. New York, NY: Oxford University Press.

Davidson, D., McKinsey, J. C. C., & Suppes, P. (1955). Outlines of a formal theory of value: I. *Philosophy of Science, 22*, 140–160.

Davidson, D., Suppes, P., & Siegel, S. (1957). *Decision making: An experimental approach*. Midway reprint 1977. Chicago, IL: University of Chicago Press.

Ferrario, R., & Schiaffonati, V. (2012). *Formal methods and empirical practices: Conversations with Patrick Suppes*. Stanford, CA: CSLO Publications.

Garcia de la Sienra, A. (2011). Suppes' methodology of economics. *Theoria, 72*, 347–366.

Giere, R. (1999). *Science without laws*. Chicago, IL: University of Chicago Press.

Grüne-Yanoff, T. (Ed.). (2009). Economic models as credible worlds or as isolating tools? *Erkenntnis, 70*, 1–131.

Harsanyi, J. (1977). *Rational behavior and bargaining equilibrium in games and social situations*. Cambridge: Cambridge University Press.

Krantz, D. H., Luce, D. R., Suppes, P., & Tversky, A. (1971/1989/1990). *Foundations of measurement*. New York, NY: Academic Press.

Mäki, U. (2013). Contested modeling: The case of economics. In U. Gähde, S. Hartmann, & J. H. Wolf (Eds.), *Models, simulations, and the reduction of complexity* (pp. 87–116). Berlin: Walter DeGruyter.

Morgan, M. (2012). *The world in the model: How economists work and think*. Cambridge: Cambridge University Press.

Morgan, M. S., & Knuuttila, T. (2012). Models and modelling in economics. In U. Mäki (Ed.), *Handbook of the philosophy of science, Vol. 13, philosophy of economics* (pp. 49–87). Amsterdam: Elsevier.

Stegmüller, W., Balzer, W., & Spohn, W. (Eds.). (1982). *Philosophy of economics*. New York, NY: Springer-Verlag.

Sugden, R. (2000). Credible worlds: The status of theoretical models in economics. *Journal of Economic Methodology, 7*, 1–31.

Suppes, P. (1960). A comparison of the meaning and uses of models in mathematic and the empirical sciences. *Synthese, 12*, 287–301.

Suppes, P. (1962). Models of data. In E. Nagel, P. Suppes, & A. Tarski (Eds.), *Logic, methodology, and philosophy of science: Proceedings of the 1960 international congress* (pp. 252–261). Stanford, CA: Stanford University Press.

Suppes, P. (1966). Some formal models of grading principles. *Synthese, 6*, 284–306.

Suppes, P. (1967). What is a scientific theory? In S. Morgenbesser (Ed.), *Philosophy of science today* (pp. 55–67). New York, NY: Basic Books.

Suppes, P. (1970). *A probabilistic theory of causality*. Amsterdam: North-Holland.

Suppes, P. (1979). Self-profile. In R. J. Bogdan (Ed.), *Patrick Suppes* (pp. 3–56). Dordrecht: D. Reidel.

Suppes, P. (1984). *Probabilistic metaphysics*. Oxford: Basil Blackwell.

Suppes, P. (1996). The nature of measurement of freedom. *Social Choice and Welfare, 13*, 183–200.

Suppes, P. (2001). Rationality, habits and freedom. In N. Dimitri, M. Basili, & I. Gilboa (Eds.), *Cognitive processes and economic behavior* (pp. 137–167). New York, NY: Routlege.

Suppes, P., & Atkinson, R. C. (1960). *Markov learning models for multiperson interactions*. Stanford, CA: Stanford University Press.

Suppes, P., & Carlsmith, J. M. (1962). Experimental analysis of a duopoly situation from the standpoint of mathematical learning theory. *International Economic Review, 3*, 60–78.

Suppes, P., & Winet, M. (1955). An axiomatization of utility based on the notion of utility differences. *Management Science, 1*, 259–270.

Suppes, P., & Zinnes, J. L. (1963). Basic measurement theory. In R. D. Luce, R. R. Bush, & E. Galanter (Eds.), *Handbook of mathematical psychology* (Vol. I, pp. 1–76). New York, NY: Wiley.

Weisberg, M. (2013). *Simulation and similarity: Using models to understand the world*. Oxford: Oxford University Press.

Patrick Suppes and game theory

Ken Binmore

This article is a contribution to a symposium celebrating the life of Patrick Suppes. It describes the context in which he made contributions relevant to two extremes of the game theory spectrum. At one extreme, he made an experimental study of whether laboratory subjects learn to use Von Neumann's minimax theory in games of pure conflict. At the other extreme, he invented a theory of empathetic identification that lies at the root of an approach to making interpersonal comparisons needed for the study of games in which cooperation is central rather than conflict. These pieces of work are peripheral to his major interests, but they nevertheless illustrate how it is possible to be an academic success without conceding anything to current academic fashion.

1. Introduction

Where should the line be drawn between philosophy and science? Aristotle and Descartes seemingly saw no reason to draw a line at all. Nor did Galileo or Newton. So Patrick Suppes was in good company when he wrote on whatever topic took his fancy with little regard either to disciplinary boundaries or to academic fashion.

To appreciate the range of interests of this extraordinary man, it is necessary to review the whole spectrum of work covered in the symposium in his honor of which this paper is a part. Here, we only look at two of his pioneering contributions that are relevant to game theory.

It is typical of Patrick Suppes that he was working on these issues in the late 1950s and early 1960s when game theory was at its lowest ebb – after the initial enthusiasm that greeted the 1944 publication of Von Neumann and Morgenstern's (1944) *Theory of Games and Economic Behavior* had dissipated into disillusion, and before there was an inkling of the revival of the late 1970s that would convert the original theory into a workhorse that is now regarded as the fundamental tool in economic theory. I do not think it would be useful for me to discuss the contents of the two pieces of work in detail since the world has moved on a great deal since those early days. Instead, I propose to review the context in which they were written and what the literature has to say about these issues in the present.

2. Zero-sum games

The first piece of work is described in a book *Applications of a Markov Model to Multiperson Interactions* written with Richard Atkinson, which belongs in a list of pioneering works in at least three areas (Suppes & Atkinson, 1958, 1960).

The first area to which it makes a contribution is the Psychology of Learning. A few years before Suppes and Atkinson's (1958) original publication, the psychologists Bush and Mosteller (1955) published a book documenting their research at the University of Michigan into stochastic models of stimulus-response learning. Their finding was that such models can be surprisingly effective in tracking the behavior over time of laboratory subjects engaged in simple tasks. However, their research was not embraced with open arms by the psychology profession at the time, presumably because their approach seemed too much like the philosophical version of behaviorism promoted by Watson and Skinner, whose initial sky-high reputation was already falling into disrepute.[1] Unconcerned with such worldly considerations, Suppes and Atkinson exploited their comparative advantage in mathematical matters to formulate their own stochastic versions of stimulus-response learning models, which they then ambitiously set out to test experimentally in multi-person situations, thereby arguably initiating the subject of Evolutionary Economics, on which there is now a very large literature (Roth).

The multi-person interactions in Suppes and Atkinson's experiments were framed as zero-sum games, and it is this aspect of their work on which I shall focus. Does Von Neumann's minimax theory of rational play in two-person zero-sum games work in practice? In seeking to answer such a question, Suppes has to be counted as one of the founders of the now flourishing subject of Experimental Economics.

2.1. Minimax theory

A game is being played whenever the actions of different people interact so that the players have to take account of the strategies that other players may choose when making their own choice of a strategy. In games of pure coordination, what is good for one player is good for them all, and so the problem the players face is how best to cooperate in order to achieve an outcome that all agree is optimal. Zero-sum games are games of pure conflict that lie at the other end of the cooperative spectrum. They are games in which the interests of the two players (Alice and Bob) are diametrically opposed, so that whatever is good for one is bad for the other. Chess and Poker are typical examples.

Von Neumann and Morgenstern's (1944) book is divided into two parts. The first part is a rigorous analysis of zero-sum games, which establishes that rational players in such games will each randomize their choice of strategy so as to achieve their maximin expected pay-off. Alice's randomized choice of strategy will then maximize her average pay-off on the assumption that Bob will successfully predict what she is doing and act to minimize her average pay-off on the assumption that his prediction is correct.[2] When both players use maximin strategies in a zero-sum game, the result is a Nash equilibrium, which means that each player is making a personally best reply to the strategy of the other.[3]

2.2. Perfect rationality?

Economists of the 1950s were sold on a methodology that treated people as rational optimizers no matter how difficult it might be to work out what strategy might be optimal. In their defense, this methodology turns out to generate predictions that work exceedingly well in the perfectly competitive markets with which they were mostly concerned in those days. Nowadays we recognize that people are subject to all kinds of irrational biases and computational inadequacies, and the reason that idealizations of neoclassical economics sometimes work well is that market institutions provide an evolutionary environment in which trial-and-error experimentation can lead to very fast convergence on a Nash equilibrium in which everybody ends up behaving as if they had worked out the optimal thing to do by rational computation. The Chicago wheat market is a stereotypical example.

But things are not so easy in zero-sum games. In the first place, the reasoning that leads to the use of a maximin strategy is a lot more complicated than the 'buy cheap and sell dear' philosophy that makes markets work. This point is nicely illustrated by the fact that Von Neumann was anticipated in the study of zero-sum games by the great mathematician Emile Borel. The record shows that Borel formulated the Minimax Theorem but decided that it was probably false. It would therefore seem pointless to run experiments designed to test the hypothesis that laboratory subjects are capable of duplicating Von Neumann's reasoning. Insofar as Von Neumann's minimax theory succeeds in predicting the behavior of laboratory subjects playing zero-sum games, it is not because they are all cleverer than Emile Borel! It is because their trial-and-error attempts to improve their past play converge on the minimax outcome. But under what conditions will such convergence occur, if at all? And how long will it take? One certainly cannot hope for the fast convergence observed in some markets that allows the appearance of rational behavior to seem almost simultaneous with the onset of trading.

But this is what economists thought they should be looking for when experimental economics had finally become respectable in the late 1980s, and some pioneers turned their attention to zero-sum games. It is therefore not surprising that their experimental results were distant from the minimax prediction (except in games like Matching Pennies for which such an outcome is easily explained on other grounds).[4] The exception was a paper with repeated play by O'Neill (1987) that he found hard to get published because it was out of line with the current literature. When finally published, it was denounced by Brown and Rosenthal (1990) on the grounds that it failed a test which treated any evidence that the players were learning to play their maximin strategies as evidence *against* Von Neumann's theory![5]

This wave of experimentation on zero-sum games came some 30 years after the original wave of which the paper by Suppes and Atkinson was a part.[6] The results of this earlier wave were no more supportive of the minimax hypothesis than the later wave, but what we know now is that if Suppes and Atkinson had been able to present their games to their subjects with computerized graphic displays (instead of using a pencil-and-paper implementation) and understood that it makes a difference whether you pay your subjects for their efforts, then their design would have supported minimax. The reason is that their design got the two important things right. Their experiment made provision for adequate trial-and-error learning, and their subjects were told in a user-friendly way precisely what game they were playing.

None of the second wave – not even O'Neill – were safe on the first point. As for the second point, the very first experiment on zero-sum games was carried out by the distinguished psychologist Estes (1957) who reported that the minimax theory may have theoretical virtues but it has no practical application. However, his subjects did not even know they were playing another human being. Even if they guessed that they were playing a game, they did not know its payoffs. In particular, they did not know the game was zero-sum. So why should they play minimax?

My own contribution to the experimental literature on zero-sum games followed the second wave mentioned above (Binmore, 2007; Binmore, Swierzbinski, & Proulx, 2001). My co-authors and I ticked all the necessary boxes by following the methodology of Suppes and Atkinson using modern experimental techniques, and so obtained results that support the minimax hypothesis. However, as with O'Neill, our paper was initially rejected, partly because our results were not consistent with the accepted literature, but mostly because we took issue with the test of Brown and Rosenthal that had become standard by this time. However, when we finally got round to submitting a revised version several years later, the whole atmosphere had changed because of the appearance in the interim of several other papers in which convergence on the Nash equilibria of a variety of games had been demonstrated in laboratory experiments. Nowadays it is well established that adequately motivated subjects given adequate time for trial-and-error learning in games with a unique Nash equilibrium will eventually converge on the Nash equilibrium most of the time.[7] Evolutionary biologists have found that corresponding results in games played by animals can sometimes be very successful in explaining behavior that would otherwise be very mysterious (Pollock, Cabrales, Rissing, & Binmore, 2012). Indeed, such biological field studies are arguably the area in which game theory has made its greatest contributions to scientific endeavor.

In summary, Patrick Suppes deserves to be credited as a pioneer in the Psychology of Learning, in Evolutionary Economics, and in Experimental Economics.

3. Comparing utilities

The second part of Von Neumann and Morgenstern's (1944) book is also mostly about zero-sum games, but in multi-person situations that are distant from the two-person games of pure conflict studied in its first part. The emphasis now is on cooperation. The players are assumed to be able to agree on binding pre-play contracts on how the game will be played. Axioms are then proposed that supposedly govern the nature of such contracts for rational players.

While Suppes was engaged in experiments on two-person zero-sum games in the 1950s and 1960s, those few scholars who retained an interest in game theory were mostly working on developing variants of Von Neumann and Morgenstern's axioms – a field that become known as cooperative game theory (as opposed to noncooperative game theory, in which pre-play contracts are not permitted and the basic concept is that of a Nash equilibrium, as in the theory of two-person zero-sum games). An immediate problem is how players' pay-offs or utilities are to be compared when pre-play contracts are being negotiated.[8]

The second part of Von Neumann and Morgenstern's (1944) book not only takes it for granted that interpersonal comparisons of utility can be made, but that players can trade units of utility (utils) between them. The assumption that utils can be traded is a step too far for most modern critics, but the idea that utils can sensibly be compared across individuals is now a routine assumption, although it was once hotly denied that such comparisons could ever be meaningful. If this were true, I share the view expressed by Hammond (1976), Harsanyi (1955) and many others that rational ethics would then become a subject with little or no substantive content.

In the remainder of this article, I plan to review the assumptions that Harsanyi (1977) added to Von Neumann and Morgenstern's (1944) theory of expected utility to justify interpersonal comparisons of utility. In Harsanyi's approach, they arise from the study of what I call empathetic preferences (Binmore, 2005). Such preferences originate with Patrick Suppes' (1966) 'Some Formal Models of Grading Principles', and were studied by Sen (1970) and Arrow (1978) under the name of 'extended sympathy preferences' before being taken up by Harsanyi.

3.1. What is utility?

The word *utility* has always been difficult. Even the archutilitarian Jeremy Bentham (1987) opens his *Principles of Morals and Legislation* by remarking that his earlier work would have been better understood if he had used *happiness* or *felicity* instead. Bentham's position, later taken up by John Stuart Mill, is that utility should be interpreted as the balance of pleasure and pain experienced by an individual human being.

Victorian economists adopted Bentham's idea and incorporated it into their models without paying much attention to its doubtful philosophical and psychological foundations. However, once economists discovered (in the 'marginalist revolution' of the early part of the twentieth century) that they did not need to attribute utility functions to economic agents in order to prove most of the propositions that seemed important at the time, all of the baggage on utility theory inherited from the Victorian era was swept away. By the late 1930s, it had become fashionable for economists to denounce cardinal utility theory as meaningless nonsense.[9] Even now, the jeremiads to this effect of the immensely influential Lionel Robbins (1938) are still occasionally quoted. It is characteristic that when Suppes made his contribution to this subject in the 1960s, Robbin's views were almost unchallenged in the economics profession.

Modern philosophers largely share Robbins' misapprehension that utilities are necessarily measures of pain or pleasure, so that comparing utilities between individuals is like quantifying how much more Alice suffers in the dentist's chair than Bob. Such a misinterpretation of the modern neoclassical concept of utility is sometimes referred to as the Causal Utility Fallacy because it takes for granted that Alice chooses *a* over *b* *because* her utility for *a* exceeds her utility for *b*. However, the modern Theory of Revealed Preference[10] disclaims any explanatory role and settles for a merely descriptive role. In particular, modern economists assign a utility function to Alice with $u(a) > u(b)$ because – for whatever reason – she would choose *a* over *b* if the opportunity arose.

Modern utility theory famously began when Oskar Morgenstern turned up at Von Neumann's house in Princeton one day in the early 1940s complaining that they didn't have a proper basis for the pay-offs in the book they were then writing together. So Von Neumann invented a theory on the spot that measures how much a rational person wants something by the size of the risk he or she is willing to take to get it. The rationality assumptions built into Von Neumann's theory simply require that people make decisions in a consistent way, but his conclusions are surprisingly strong. Anyone who chooses consistently in risky situations will look to an observer as though he or she were trying to maximize the average value of something. This abstract 'something' is what is called utility in the modern theory.

3.2. Comparing utils

Why does a rich man hail a taxicab when it rains while a poor man gets wet? Economists answer this traditional question by making an intrapersonal comparison. They argue that an extra dollar in Alice's pocket would be worth more to her if she were poor than it would be if she were rich. But how are we to quantify such a comparison? The answer offered by the Von Neumann and Morgenstern theory is that we can count the number of utils by which her total utility is increased when she gains an extra dollar. Because a rational decision-maker in the Von Neumann and Morgenstern theory acts as though maximizing average utility, she behaves as though each util is 'worth' the same as any other.

But what of the utils acquired by a rational Bob? In the absence of a Tiresias with experience of both roles, to whom do we appeal when asked to compare Alice and Bob's utils? The rationality postulates of Von Neumann and Morgenstern provide no justification for such comparisons – which fact provided extra ammunition for the die-hard followers of Robbbins in denying that rational interpersonal comparison is possible at all. However, as Harsanyi pointed out, what is to prevent our adding further postulates that do allow interpersonal comparison? Harsanyi's (1977) additional assumptions are built on the notion of what I call empathetic preferences as introduced by Patrick Suppes (1966).

In surveying the history of utilitarianism, Russell Hardin (1988) dismisses Hume's emphasis on the importance of sympathetic identification between human beings as idiosyncratic. Although Adam Smith (1975) followed his teacher in making human sympathy a major plank in his *Theory of Moral Sentiments*, Hardin is doubtless broadly right in judging that later moral philosophers appeal to human sympathy only when in need of some auxiliary support for a conclusion to which they were led largely by other considerations. Suppes was therefore again treading where others chose not to go.

What Hume and Adam Smith called sympathy is nowadays usually known as *empathy;* psychologists tend to reserve the word *sympathy* for a stronger notion. Alice empathizes with Bob when she imagines herself in his shoes in order to see things from his point of view. She sympathizes with Bob when she identifies with him so strongly that she is unable to separate her interests from his. The theory of revealed preference has no difficulty in describing Alice's behavior in such a case of sympathetic identification. One simply writes altruistic (or spiteful) preferences into her utility function.

It is easy to see why the forces of biological evolution might lead to our behaving as though we were equipped with sympathetic preferences. Mothers commonly care for their children more than they do for themselves. In such basic matters as these, it seems that we differ little from crocodiles or spiders. However, humans do not sympathize only with their children; it is uncontroversial that they also sympathize to varying degrees, with their husbands and wives, with their extended families, with their friends and neighbors, and with their sect or tribe. Modern behavioral economists are willing to proceed as though we all sympathize with everybody to much the same degree that we sympathize with our near and dear. If this were true, then the Von Neumann and Morgenstern theory would be adequate all by itself to determine a standard of interpersonal comparison, because Alice would only need to consult her own sympathetic utility function to find out how many utils to assign to a change in Bob's situation as compared with some change in her own situation. But Harsanyi's (1977) approach is less naive. He argues that, alongside our personal preferences (which may or may not include sympathetic concerns for others), we also have empathetic preferences that reflect our ethical concerns.

3.3. Empathetic preferences

When Alice *empathizes* with Bob, she does not necessarily identify with him so closely that she ceases to separate her own preferences from his. We weep, for example, with

Romeo when he believes Juliet to be dead. We understand why he takes his own life – but we feel no particular inclination to join him in the act. Similarly, a confidence trickster is unlikely to sympathize with his victims, but he will be very much more effective at extracting money from them if he is able to put himself in their shoes with a view to predicting how they will respond to his overtures. I think we unconsciously carry out such feats of empathetic identification on a routine basis when playing the game of life each day with our fellow citizens.

It seems evident to me that empathetic identification is crucial to the survival of human societies. It provides a tool for predicting the behavior of those around us, and so helps us find our way to equilibria in the games we play that would otherwise require a slow and clumsy process of trial and error. However, it is not enough for the viability of a human society that we be able to use empathetic identification to recognize the equilibria of commonly occurring games. The games we play often have large numbers of equilibria. As Hume (1978) saw several hundred years ago and Schelling (1960) and Lewis (1969) have emphasized in modern times, society therefore needs commonly understood coordinating conventions that select a particular equilibrium when many are available. Sometimes the conventions that have evolved are essentially arbitrary, as in the case of the side of the road on which we drive. However, in circumstances that are more deeply rooted in our social history, we usually overlook the conventional nature of our equilibrium selection criteria. We internalize the criteria so successfully that we fail to notice that selection criteria are in use at all.

I think we are particularly prone to such sleepwalking when using those conventional rules that we justify with airy references to 'fairness' when asked to explain our behavior. In saying this, I do not have in mind the rhetorical appeals to fairness that typify wage negotiations or debates over taxation. Nor do I have in mind the abstract notions of justice proposed by philosophers like Rawls (1972). I am thinking rather of the give-and-take of ordinary life. Who should wash the dishes tonight? Who ought to buy the next round of drinks? How long is it reasonable to allow a bore to monopolize the conversation over the dinner table? We are largely unconscious of the fairness criteria we use to resolve such questions, but the degree of consensus that we achieve in so doing is really quite remarkable.

Many attempts have been made to model the fairness norms we use to solve the equilibrium selection problems posed by the multitude of coordination games of which our daily social life largely consists. When such fairness norms take account of the fact that different people have different preferences,[11] they necessarily require some degree of empathetic identification.

The leading proposal for such a fairness norm is Rawls' (1972) device of the original position, which was independently proposed by Harsanyi (1977) at around the same time. To work out what is fair using this device, Alice and Bob should imagine the bargaining outcome they would reach if their identities were concealed behind a 'veil of ignorance' that gave neither any more reason than the other to think themselves Alice or Bob. Both Rawls and Harsanyi offer a Kantian defense of the original position, but my guess is that the real reason the original position appeals so strongly to our intuition is that, in working through its implications, we recognize that it epitomizes the basic principle that underlies the fairness criteria that have evolved to adjudicate our day-to-day interactions with our fellows.

A fairness norm like the original position would obviously be worthless if one person were to imagine how it would feel to be another person without substituting the other person's personal preferences for their own. But more than this is necessary.

In order to make fairness judgments, people must be able to say *how much* better or worse they feel when identifying with others. Empathetic identification by itself is not sufficient for this purpose. An essential prerequisite for the use of a device like the original position is that we be equipped with the empathetic *preferences* introduced by Suppes (1966).

It seems uncontentious that we actually do have empathetic preferences that we reveal when we make fairness judgments. Ordinary folk are doubtless less than consistent in the empathetic preferences they reveal, but Harsanyi (1977) idealized the situation by taking *homo economicus* as his model of man. In his model, everybody therefore has consistent empathetic preferences, which Harsanyi takes to mean that they satisfy the Von Neumann and Morgenstern rationality postulates. An empathetic preference can then be described using a Von Neumann and Morgenstern utility function.

An orthodox personal utility function of the kind we have considered hitherto simply assigns a utility to each situation that the person in question might encounter. For an empathetic utility function we have to pair up each such situation with the person whom we are considering in that situation. One such pair might consist of Alice drinking a cup of coffee. Another might be Bob eating a doughnut. An empathetic utility function assigns a utility to each such pair. It is, of course, precisely such pairs of possibilities that must be evaluated when people imagine themselves in the original position behind a veil of ignorance that hypothetically conceals their identity. That is to say, in the case of only two people, the set of outcomes that need to be evaluated in the original position is a bunch of possibilities of which one might be that Alice ends up with a cup of coffee and Bob with a doughnut.

The next step in Harsanyi's argument is another idealization. He assumes that when people empathize with Alice or Bob, they do so entirely successfully. More precisely, if Bob is totally successful in empathizing with Alice, then the preferences he will express when imagining myself in Alice's position will be identical to Alice's own personal preferences.

The rest of Harsanyi's argument is a straightforward application of the properties of Von Neumann and Morgenstern utility functions. The property that matters here is that any two Von Neumann and Morgenstern utility scales that represent exactly the same preferences over risky alternatives must be related in the same way as two temperature scales. That is to say, the two scales can differ only in the placing of their zero and their unit. For example, once one knows the number of degrees that the Centigrade and Fahrenheit scales assign to the freezing and boiling points of water, then one knows how to translate any temperature on one scale into the corresponding temperature on the other scale.

The two utility scales to which this fact is now applied are Alice's personal scale and an observer's empathetic scale for Alice. Since Harsanyi's second assumption implies that both scales represent the same preferences, the observer's empathetic scale for Alice is exactly the same as her personal scale except that the zero and the unit are changed. In particular, a util on the observer's empathetic scale for Alice is obtained by multiplying a util on her personal scale by some constant number a. Similarly, a util on the observer's empathetic scale for Bob is obtained by multiplying a util on her personal scale by some constant number b.

It follows that the observer's empathetic utility function simply expresses the fact that the observer thinks that Alice and Bob's personal utils can be traded off so that a of Alice's personal utils count the same as b of Bob's personal utils. That is to say,

Harsanyi's assumptions imply that holding an empathetic preference is exactly the same thing as subscribing to a standard for making interpersonal comparisons.

3.4. Utilitarianism?

One slots this theory of interpersonal comparison into the standard theory of revealed preference by assuming that our observer makes fairness judgments in a consistent way, and that we know enough of these fairness judgments to be able to summarize all of them in a single empathetic utility function. Harsanyi (1977) continues by postulating an Ideal Observer (like that of Adam Smith), whose judgments are assumed to be 'morally binding.' Since the Ideal Observer's empathetic utility function satisfies the Von Neumann and Morgenstern postulates, the Ideal Observer makes decisions by maximizing the average value of this function. Harsanyi thereby provides the kind of formal defense of utilitarianism that is usually attributed to John Stuart Mill, but is nowhere to be found in his work.

3.5. Evolutionary ethics

In my own work (Binmore, 2005), I follow Harsanyi's theory of interpersonal comparison, but I balk at the introduction of an Ideal Observer, whose hypothetical fairness judgments are somehow 'morally binding'. I prefer Harsanyi's second defense of utilitarianism, in which he joins Rawls in replacing his Ideal Observer by the device of the original position. But my impatience with metaphysical defenses of ethical concepts leads me to continue by asking why we should find the notion of the original position intuitive in the first place. And, given that the original position is to be used, how come we all employ the *same* standard of interpersonal comparison?

My evolutionary answers to these questions do not find favor with orthodox moral philosophers, but the arguments I offer suggest that the fairness norms which actually work in practice originally evolved as equilibrium selection devices in the game of life that our ancestors played on a daily basis in the far past. If I am right, fairness norms share with language the property that their deep structure is universal in the human species, but their surface structure differs from one society to another. Both biological and cultural evolution must therefore be taken into account. I go on to offer reasons why the deep structure of fairness norms should coincide with the original position, but argue that the standard of interpersonal comparison needed to operationalize the original position should be expected to vary not only with culture but also with context.

Within such a naturalistic framework, nothing binds anybody to anything, and so Harsanyi's defense of utilitarianism fails.[12] One is led instead to an alternative concept from cooperative game theory called the egalitarian or proportional bargaining solution, which might be said to formalize Aristotle's observation that 'What is fair ... is what is proportional.'

4. Conclusion

Patrick Suppes was a scholar like Epicurus or Hume, who delighted in being part of a circle of philosophers in which no subjects were taboo – anything could be discussed without anybody getting upset or feeling patronized. This article looks only at two rather special contributions he made to game theory, but even here his disregard for academic fashion when on the track of something interesting is evident. Nor did age curb his enthusiasm or blunt his joy in a good argument. I hope this symposium will give some feeling, not only of the wide breadth of his interests, but of the pleasure those who knew him took in his company.

Disclosure statement

No potential conflict of interest was reported by the author.

Notes

1. The behaviorism of Watson and Skinner needs to be sharply distinguished from the behavioral economics associated with the names of Kahneman and Tversky.
2. Von Neumann's (1928) Minimax Theorem says that a player's minimax and maximin pay-offs are equal when players are allowed to randomize. But it does not follow – as one sometimes reads – that rational players should choose their minimax strategies rather than their maximin strategies.
3. General games often have many Nash equilibria among which it can be difficult to make a rational choice, but all Nash equilibria in two-person zero-sum games are interchangeable and pay-off equivalent so that no equilibrium selection problem arises.
4. For example, Rapaport and Boebel (1992), Mookherjee and Sopher (1994, 1997), McCabe, Mukherji, and Runcie (1994).
5. Because maximin players will randomize *independently* each time they play, but the choices of players who are learning will be correlated as they find their way to equilibrium.
6. The other papers were by Frenkel (1973), Estes (1957) and Malcolm and Lieberman (1965).
7. A few behavioral economists deny this fact, even in the case of the Prisoners' Dilemma where the evidence is overwhelmingly strong (see Ledyard's, 1995 survey of the very large literature).
8. The same problem does not arise in two-person zero-sum games, for which it is only necessary that the players have opposing preferences over all pairs of alternatives. Their utility functions can then be normalized to add up to zero without assuming anything about the relative strength of their preferences.
9. A cardinal utility scale operates like a temperature scale, with utils replacing degrees. It is normally contrasted with an ordinal utility scale, in which the amount by which the utility of one outcome exceeds the utility of another outcome is held to be meaningless.
10. I would prefer to say the Theory of Attributed Preference.
11. So that Alice needs to qualify the Golden Rule – that she should do unto Bob as she would that he do unto her – by accepting that his preferences may not be same as hers.
12. Without any need to follow Rawls in his iconoclastic denial of orthodox Bayesian decision theory. However, once governments appear on the scene as enforcement agencies, Harsanyi's arguments for utilitarianism can be revived.

References

Arrow, K. (1978). Extended sympathy and the problem of social choice. *Philosophia, 7*, 233–237.
Bentham, J. (1987). An introduction to the principles of morals and legislation. In *Utilitarianism and other essays*. Harmondsworth: Penguin. (In Introduction by A. Ryan. Essay first published 1789).
Binmore, K. (2005). *Natural justice*. New York, NY: Oxford University Press.
Binmore, K. (2007). *Does game theory work? The bargaining challenge*. Cambridge, MA: MIT Press.
Binmore, K., Swierzbinski, J., & Proulx, C. (2001). Does minimax work? An experimental study. *Economic Journal, 111*, 445–465.
Brown, J., & Rosenthal, R. (1990). Testing the minimax hypothesis: A re-examination of O'Neill's game experiment. *Econometrica, 58*, 1065–1081.
Bush, R., & Mosteller, F. (1955). *Stochastic models for learning*. New York, NY: Wiley.

Estes, W. (1957). Of models and men. *American Psychologist, 12*, 609–617.

Frenkel, O. (1973). *A study of 78 non-iterated 2 × 2 games* (Staff Report 176). Minneapolis: Federal Reserve Bank of Minneapolis.

Hammond, P. (1976). Why ethical measures of inequality need interpersonal comparisons. *Theory and Decision, 7*, 263–274.

Hardin, R. (1988). *Morality within the limits of reason*. Chicago, IL: University of Chicago Press.

Harsanyi, J. (1955). Cardinal welfare, individualistic ethics, and interpersonal comparisons of utility. *Journal of Political Economy, 63*, 309–321.

Harsanyi, J. (1977). *Rational behavior and bargaining equilibrium in games and social situations*. Cambridge: Cambridge University Press.

Hume, D. (1978). *A treatise of human nature* (2nd ed.). (Edited by L. A. Selby-Bigge, Revised by P. Nidditch. First published 1739). Oxford: Clarendon Press.

Ledyard, J. (1995). Public goods: A survey of experimental research. In J. Kagel & A. Roth (Eds.), *Handbook of experimental economics* (pp. 111–181). Princeton, NJ: Princeton University Press.

Lewis, D. (1969). *Conventions: A philosophical study*. Cambridge, MA: Harvard University Press.

Malcolm, D., & Lieberman, B. (1965). The behavior of responsive individuals playing a two-person zero-sum game. *Psychonomic Science, 2*, 373–374.

McCabe, K., Mukherji, A., & Runcie, D. (1994). *An experimental study of learning and limited information in games* (Staff Report 176). Minneapolis: Federal Reserve Bank of Minneapolis.

Mookherjee, D., & Sopher, B. (1994). *An experimental study of learning and limited information in constant-sum games* (Technical Report). New Brunswick, NJ: Rutgers University.

Mookherjee, D., & Sopher, B. (1997). Learning and decision costs in experimental constant-sum games. *Games and Economic Behavior, 19*, 62–91.

O'Neill, B. (1987). Nonmetric test of the minimax theory of two-person zerosum games. *Proceedings of the National Academy of Sciences, 84*, 2106–2109.

Pollock, G., Cabrales, A., Rissing, S., & Binmore, K. (2012). Suicidal punishment in the ant *Acromyrmex Versicolor. Evolutionary Ecological Research, 14*, 1–21.

Rapoport, A., & Budescu, D. (1992). Generation of random series in two-person strictly competitive games. *Journal of Experimental Psychology: General, 121*, 352–363.

Rawls, J. (1972). *A theory of justice*. Oxford: Oxford University Press.

Robbins, L. (1938). Interpersonal comparisons of utility: A comment. *The Economic Journal, 48*, 635–641.

Roth, A. *Bibliography of learning in games: Theory, experiment, and related subjects*. Retrieved from web.stanford.edu/'alroth/learnbib.html

Schelling, T. (1960). *The strategy of conflict*. Cambridge, MA: Harvard University Press.

Sen, A. (1970). *Collective choice and social welfare*. San Francisco, CA: Holden Day.

Smith, A. (1975). *The theory of moral sentiments*. Oxford: Clarendon Press. (Edited by D. Raphael & A. Macfie. First published 1759).

Suppes, P. (1966). Some formal models of grading principles. *Synthese, 16*, 284–306.

Suppes, P., & Atkinson, R. (1958). An analysis of two-person game situations in terms of statistical learning theory. *Journal of Experimental Psychology, 55*, 369–378.

Suppes, P., & Atkinson, R. (1960). *Applications of a Markov model to multiperson interactions*. Stanford, CA: Stanford University Press.

Von Neumann, J. (1928). Zur Theorie der Gesellschaftsspiele. *Mathematische Annalen, 100*, 295–320.

Von Neumann, J., & Morgenstern, O. (1944). *The theory of games and economic behavior*. Princeton, NJ: Princeton University Press.

Measurement theory and utility analysis in Suppes' early work, 1951–1958

Ivan Moscati

The paper reconstructs the connections between the evolution of Patrick Suppes' measurement theory from 1951 to 1958 and the research in utility analysis he conducted between 1953 and 1957 within the Stanford Value Theory Project. In particular, the paper shows that Suppes' superseding of the classical understanding of measurement, his endorsement of the representational view of measurement, and his conceiving of an axiomatic version of the latter were prompted by his research in utility analysis.

1. Introduction

In the historiography of measurement theory, it is customary to distinguish between the 'classical' and the 'representational' concepts of measurement. The former is labeled 'classical' because it dates back to Aristotle and dominated philosophy and science until the early decades of the twentieth century. The 'representational' view of measurement subsumes the classical view as a special case. It emerged in the first half of the twentieth century, primarily to account for the methods used in experimental psychology to quantify sensations, and was originally articulated by the Harvard psychologist Stanley Smith Stevens in 1946 (see e.g. Michell, 1999; Moscati, 2013a).

Both conceptions of measurement were, at some point, axiomatized. A first axiomatic version of the classical view was put forward by Otto Hölder (1901/1996); other versions were subsequently advanced by, among others, Suppes (1951) in his first published article. The axiomatic approach to the representational view of measurement was outlined by Suppes and Dana Scott (1958), developed by Suppes and Joseph Zinnes in a chapter of the *Handbook of Mathematical Psychology* (1963), and found its full-fledged expression in *Foundations of Measurement*, the book Suppes wrote in collaboration with David H. Krantz, R. Duncan Luce, and Amos Tversky and the first volume of which was published in 1971. In recent years, the axiomatic version of the representational view of measurement elaborated by Suppes and his co-authors has been criticized for paying inadequate attention to the empirical dimension of measurement (Boumans, 2015; Frigerio, Giordani, & Mari, 2010). However, it still represents the standard approach in measurement theory, and even scholars who are critical of it take the *Foundations of Measurement* as the starting point of their research.

In an autobiographical essay, Suppes (1979, pp. 13–16) recalled that the evolution of his view on measurement between 1951 and 1958 was driven by the work in utility analysis he conducted within the Stanford Value Theory Project between 1953 and 1957. So far as I am aware, however, there exists no systematic study of Suppes' early work in measurement theory and utility analysis that reconstructs in detail the connections between these two threads of his research. The present paper fills this lacuna, and shows how Suppes' superseding of the classical understanding of measurement, his endorsement of the representational view, and his conceiving of an axiomatic version of the latter were all prompted by his investigations in collaboration with Chen McKinsey, Donald Davidson, Muriel Winet, and Sidney Siegel at the Stanford Value Theory Project.

When Suppes entered utility analysis in the early 1950s, most research in the field was building on *Theory of Games and Economic Behavior*, the book mathematician John von Neumann and economist Oskar Morgenstern had published in 1944 (second edition 1947, third edition 1953). Besides originating modern game theory, the book made three further important contributions to economics. First, it introduced into the economic analysis of decision-making the set-theoretical axiomatic approach that was already mainstream in mathematics (Mongin, 2004). Second, it offered an axiomatic foundation to Expected Utility Theory (EUT), the theory of choices involving risk that had been adopted by early marginalists but had been subjected to sustained criticism in the 1930s and early 1940s. Between the late 1940s and early 1950s, von Neumann and Morgenstern's axiomatic version of EUT generated an intense debate in which many major economists of the period took part. By 1952–1953, however, a substantial consensus on EUT had formed, at least among American economists (Mongin, 2009; Moscati, 2016). Finally, since the expected utility formula features a cardinal utility function, i.e. a function unique up to linearly increasing transformations, the rise of EUT was associated with the rehabilitation of cardinal utility. This concept had been marginalized in the 1930s and early 1940 because it was at odds with the ordinal approach then dominant in utility analysis.[1]

Suppes' research on utility theory between 1953 and 1957 focused on the axiomatization of EUT and cardinal utility, and also on the experimental testing of EUT. In the course of this research, Suppes became aware that his axiomatizations of EUT and cardinal utility could be seen as particular instances of a more general exercise, namely that of specifying axiomatically the conditions that make a generic object – not only utility – measurable in one way rather than another. This paved the way for his axiomatization of the representational view of measurement, which he delineated in his 1958 article with Scott.

A final introductory remark is in order. Suppes wrote most of the works examined in the present paper in collaboration with other scholars (Davidson, McKinsey, Scott, Siegel, and Winet), and it is extremely difficult to disentangle his specific contributions from those of his co-authors. Therefore, in the paper I will treat each work as a joint product and assume that it fully reflected Suppes' views, as well as those of his co-authors. In fact, Suppes' co-authors dealt with measurement-theoretic issues only in those papers co-written with him, and therefore one could make the stronger case that those works reflected, first and foremost, Suppes' views on measurement. But such a strong claim is not needed for the purposes of this paper.

2. Axiomatizing classical measurement

Patrick Colonel Suppes (1922–2014) studied physics and meteorology at the University of Chicago (BS 1943) and, after serving in the Army Air Force during the war, in 1947 entered Columbia University as a graduate student in philosophy (Suppes, 1979). At Columbia, he came under the influence of the philosopher and measurement theorist Ernest Nagel, and also took courses in advanced mathematical topics. Around 1948, he was one of a group of Columbia PhD students who organized an informal seminar on von Neumann and Morgenstern's *Theory of Games*. He graduated in June 1950 under Nagel's supervision and, in September of the same year, joined the Department of Philosophy at Stanford University, where he remained for the rest of his working life.

In his first article, Suppes (1951) put forward a series of axioms that warrant the measurability of objects according to the classical conception of measurement. According to this conception, measuring the property of an object (e.g. the length of a table) consists of comparing it with some other object that displays the same property and is taken as a unit (e.g. a meter-long ruler) and then assessing the numerical ratio between the unit and the object to be measured (if the ratio is two to one, the table is two meters long). Over the course of the history of measurement theory, the key condition warranting the measurability of objects in the classical sense was identified in the possibility of adding objects in a sense analogous to that in which numbers are summed (two tables can be 'added' by placing them end to end, and the length of the resulting surface is equal to the sum of the lengths of the two single tables).

In 1901, the German mathematician Otto Hölder applied to measurement theory the axiomatic approach to geometry launched two years earlier by Hilbert (1899/1950). Hölder (1901/1996) laid down seven axioms on magnitudes and proved that, if magnitudes satisfy them, the ratio between any two magnitudes is well-defined, and one magnitude can be taken as a unit to measure the others. In other words, Hölder specified axiomatically the conditions warranting the measurability of objects in the classical sense.

Despite its importance for the theory of measurement, Hölder's article went unnoticed until the early 1930s when it was rediscovered by Nagel, who later became Suppes' mentor at Columbia. Nagel (1931) suggested a set of 12 axioms, slightly different from Hölder's, which should warrant the measurability of magnitudes in the classical sense. However, Nagel did not give any formal proof that his axioms actually deliver classical measurability.

Building on Hölder and Nagel, Suppes in his first article considered a set of objects, a binary relation between these objects interpretable as the inequality relation $\leq$, and a binary function interpretable as the operation of addition $+$. Suppes put forward seven axioms concerning the set of objects, the relation $\leq$, and the operation $+$, and proved that, although less restrictive than Hölder's, his axioms were nonetheless sufficient to warrant the measurability of the elements of the set in the classical sense.[2]

3. Stevens and the representational view of measurement

In 1951, Suppes did not refer to Stanley Smith Stevens and the representational conception of measurement the latter had expounded in 1946. Nevertheless, a brief aside on Stevens' measurement theory is in order at this point in the narrative.

For Stevens (1946, p. 677), measurement consists of 'the assignment of numerals to objects or events according to rules.' Since there are various rules for assigning numbers to objects, there are various forms, or 'scales', of measurement. Generally speaking, measurement is possible in the first place because there is 'a certain isomorphism' (p. 677), i.e. a certain similarity, between some empirical relations between the objects to be measured and some formal relations between the numbers assigned to those objects. Thus, for example, there exists an isomorphism between the empirical relation 'longer than' between tables, and the formal relation 'greater than' between numbers.

Stevens (1946, pp. 678–680) identified four basic measurement scales and characterized each one by a set of empirical operations and by the class of mathematical transformations the numbers in the scale can be subjected to without altering the scale's capacity of representing the empirical relations among objects. For instance, he characterized the interval scale by three operations: (i) the determination of whether two objects are equal with respect to some trait; (ii) the ranking of objects; (iii) the determination of equality of differences between objects. Mathematically, the interval scale is identified by linearly increasing transformations, i.e. those of the form $f(x) = \alpha x + \beta$, where α is a positive constant, and β is a constant that can also be negative.[3] As an example of interval scales in physics, Stevens considered the Centigrade and Fahrenheit scales of temperature. In economics, we may add, cardinal utility is measurable according to an interval-scale.

For Stevens, the classical conception of measurement is a narrow one which identifies measurement with a specific, and quite demanding, form of measurement, namely ratio-scale measurement. Most of the entities studied by physics and other natural disciplines can be added, and are therefore measurable according to a ratio-scale, i.e. in the classical sense. By contrast, sensations, intellectual abilities, utility, and other entities studied by the behavioral and social sciences cannot be added, and thus cannot be measured according to a ratio-scale. However, for Stevens, these entities might be subject to other empirical operations and hence measured according to other scales.

Two final comments on Stevens' representational theory of measurement are in order. First, Stevens' theory was not an axiomatic one. He associated each scale of measurement with a set of empirical operations and a class of mathematical transformations, but did not attempt to specify under what exact conditions, i.e. axioms, certain operations are feasible while others are not. Steven did not even attempt to prove mathematically how a specific class of admissible transformations draws from a given set of operations and, accordingly, there are no 'representation theorems' in his work.[4]

Second, Stevens (1946) theory of measurement displays significant similarities, but also differences, with the theory of measurement outlined by von Neumann and Morgenstern in the first chapter of *Theory of Games* (von Neumann & Morgenstern, 1944). Like Stevens, von Neumann and Morgenstern related measurement to the assignment of numbers to objects, and connected different types of measurement with different classes of mathematical transformations. However, they associated the possibility of proper measurement with the possibility of adding the objects to be measured, which confers a classical flavor to their theory of measurement.[5]

Returning to Suppes, we should note that neither his exclusive focus on the classical conception of measurement in his 1951 article nor his apparent ignorance of Stevens' measurement theory are surprising. This is because Suppes' background was not in psychology or economics, but in disciplines such as philosophy, mathematics, and physics, in which the classical conception of measurement remained unrivaled. The articles Suppes published between 1951 and 1953 also belonged to these latter disciplines. In these works, Suppes and his co-authors advanced a set-theoretical axiomatic foundation of particle mechanics (McKinsey, Sugar, & Suppes, 1953; McKinsey & Suppes, 1953a, 1953b). Regarding measurement issues, these articles remained within the orbit of the classical conception. In 1953, however, things changed rapidly.

4. The Stanford Value Theory Project

In the early 1950s, two main factors contributed to a shift in Suppes' research interests toward economics, psychology, and the behavioral sciences in general. The first factor was the influence of J.C.C. 'Chen' McKinsey, Suppes' postdoctoral tutor at Stanford. McKinsey (1908–1953) was a logician who had worked intensively on game theory at the RAND Corporation, a think tank created by the US Air Force in 1946 and located in Santa Monica, California. In 1951, McKinsey, after being forced to leave RAND because his homosexuality was considered a security risk (Nasar, 1998), joined Stanford's Philosophy Department. At the time, he was completing his *Introduction to the Theory of Games* (McKinsey, 1952), which would become the first textbook in game theory. Suppes' familiarity with game theory and decision analysis was further enhanced by his summer research position in the early 1950s, working with David Blackwell and Meyer A. Girshick while they were writing their book *Theory of Games and Statistical Decisions* (Blackwell & Girshick, 1954), in which the tools of decision theory and game theory were employed to evaluate statistical procedures.

From McKinsey, Suppes learned not only game theory, but also the set-theoretical methods that would play a crucial role in his subsequent work. McKinsey also encouraged Suppes to attend the seminar conducted by the eminent logician Alfred Tarski at the University of California at Berkeley. According to Suppes (1979, p. 8), 'it was from McKinsey and Tarski that I learned about the axiomatic method and what it means to give a set-theoretical analysis of a subject.'[6]

The second, and possibly more powerful, factor that contributed to shift Suppes' research interests toward the behavioral sciences was funding. In 1953, John Goheen, the chair of Stanford's Department of Philosophy, obtained a grant from the Ford Foundation for a study on 'Value, Decision and Rationality.' Around the same time, Goheen negotiated contracts with two military agencies, namely the Office of Naval Research and the Office of Ordnance Research of the US army, for work on the theory of decisions involving risk. Goheen entrusted McKinsey and Suppes with the project, which was renamed the 'Stanford Value Theory Project' (Isaac, 2013; Suppes, 1979).[7]

McKinsey and Suppes co-opted into the enterprise Donald Davidson, another philosopher who had joined the Philosophy Department in January 1951. Davidson (1917–2003) had studied at Harvard University (BA 1939, PhD 1949), where he was influenced by logician and analytical philosopher W.V.O. Quine. Today, Davidson is best known for his influential work on the philosophy of mind and action, the philosophy of language, and epistemology. However, he published these works only from the early 1960s on. In the 1950s, he was still very busy with teaching and did not as yet have a clear philosophical project. As he explained in a later interview: 'Suppes and McKinsey took me under their wing [...] because they thought this guy [Davidson] really ought to get some stuff out' (Lepore, 2004, p. 252).

Most of the research connected with the Stanford Value Theory Project was conducted between 1953 and 1955, and appeared in print between 1955 and 1957. The final output consisted of three articles, each of a theoretical character (Davidson, McKinsey, & Suppes, 1955; Davidson & Suppes, 1956; Suppes & Winet, 1955), and a book presenting the results of an experiment to measure the utility of money (Davidson, Suppes,

& Siegel, 1957). However, McKinsey contributed only to the setting up and very early work of the Project because in October 1953 he committed suicide.

5. Axiomatizing cardinal utility by utility differences

October 1953 is relevant for our narrative also because in that month Suppes and his doctoral student Muriel Winet completed a first version of one of the Stanford Value Theory Project papers, namely, 'An Axiomatization of Utility Based on the Notion of Utility Differences' (Suppes & Winet 1953/1954). The paper was presented in November 1953 at a meeting of the American Mathematical Society held at the California Institute of Technology, and was later published in the April–July 1955 issue of the first volume of *Management Science*, a newly founded journal that was open to studies in decision theory from different disciplines.[8] In their work, Suppes and Winet (1955) advanced an axiomatization of cardinal utility based on the assumption that individuals are not only able to rank the utility of different commodities, as is assumed in the ordinal approach to utility, but are also capable of ranking the differences between the utilities of commodities.

There are different methods for arriving at a cardinal utility function. The method popular in the early 1950s was based on the EUT axioms. As already mentioned, it was in fact through the association with EUT that cardinal utility was rehabilitated in economic theory in this period. An older way of attaining cardinal utility was based on the assumption that the utilities of different commodities are independent. However, from the 1910s the majority of utility theorists had rejected this assumption because it rules out conspicuous economic phenomena such as the complementarity and substitutability of goods. A third route, based on the ranking of utility differences, had been extensively discussed in the 1930s by Lange (1934), Phelps Brown (1934), Alt (1936/1971), Samuelson (1938) and other economists. At that time, however, most utility theorists had remained skeptical about the ranking of utility differences because it has no clear observable counterpart in terms of acts of choice, and therefore relies only upon introspection, which was not considered a reliable source of evidence (see Baccelli & Mongin, 2016; Moscati, 2013b).

Suppes and Winet (1955, p. 259) mentioned that the notion of utility differences had been already discussed in economics, and cited Lange's (1934) article on the topic. They also took a stance against the economists' opposition to introspection that, since the mid-1930s, had played a crucial role in the marginalization of utility differences in economic analysis. They claimed that in many areas of economic theory 'there is little reason to be ashamed of direct appeals to introspection', and that there are sound arguments for justifying 'the determination of utility differences by introspective methods' (p. 261). They then affirmed that, despite the importance and legitimacy of utility differences, to the best of their knowledge 'no adequate axiomatization for this difference notion has yet been given' (p. 259). Evidently, they were ignorant of the fact that almost 20 years earlier, in the debate initiated by Lange, the Viennese mathematician Alt (1936/1971) had provided a rigorous axiomatization of cardinal utility anticipating in significant respects that of Suppes and Winet.[9]

Like Alt, Suppes and Winet considered two order relations – Q and R – over the elements of an abstract set K. Q is a standard, binary preference relation: xQy means that x is not preferred to y. R is a quaternary relation concerning 'differences' or 'intervals' between alternatives: $(x,y)R(z,w)$ means that the interval between x and y is not greater than the interval between z and w. Suppes and Winet imposed 11 axioms on the set K, the relations Q and R. The conditions these axioms impose are analogous to the conditions defined by Alt: completeness, transitivity, continuity, and some form of additivity for the two order relations, and an Archimedean property on R.[10]

Based on their 11 axioms, Suppes and Winet proved what they explicitly called a 'representation theorem' (p. 265): the axioms imply the existence of a function u that can be interpreted as a utility function, is unique up to linearly increasing transformations, and is such that the interval between x and y is smaller than the interval between z and w if and only if the absolute utility difference between x and y is smaller than the absolute utility difference between z and w (pp. 265–270). More formally, xQy if and only if $u(x){\leq}u(y)$, and $(x,y)R(z,w)$, if and only if $|u(x){-}u(y)|{\leq}|u(z){-}u(w)|$.[11]

In the terminology of Stevens' representational theory of measurement, Suppes and Winet's axioms identify a set of operations that allow one to assign (utility) numbers to objects according to an interval rather than a ratio-scale. In their article, Suppes and Winet referred to two papers the Harvard psychologist had published before 1946 (Stevens, 1936; Stevens & Volkmann, 1940), but did not mention Stevens' measurement theory, did not use his scale-of-measurement terminology, and, accordingly, did not label cardinal utility as utility measurable on an interval scale.

Nevertheless, by identifying conditions that warrant the interval-scale measurement of an object, Suppes overcame the classical conception that confines measurement to ratio measurement. Suppes' superseding of the classical view of measurement and his endorsement of the representational view became more explicit in a paper he read at the annual meeting of the Pacific Division of the American Philosophical Association that was held at Stanford University in December 1953.

6. Endorsing the representational view

This paper, which does not belong to those funded by the Stanford Value Theory Project, bore the title 'Some Remarks on Problems and Methods in the Philosophy of Science,' and was published the following year in *Philosophy of Science*. In this, Suppes (1954) made various programmatic proposals for the advancement of the philosophy of science, some of which concerned the theory of measurement.

Suppes argued that the most urgent task in the philosophy of science was that of 'axiomatizing the theory of all developed braches of empirical science' (p. 244). In particular, for Suppes this axiomatization program should not be based on logic or other metamathematical languages but on set-theoretical methods:

We can pursue a program of axiomatization without constructing any formal languages. [...] The basic methods appropriate for axiomatic studies in empirical sciences are not metamathematical (and thus syntactical and semantical), but set-theoretical (p. 244).In Suppes' view, the axiomatization task could be divided into four steps: (i) listing the primitive notions of a given theory and characterizing them in set-theoretical terms; (ii) indicating the axioms that the notions must satisfy; (iii) investigating the deductive consequences of the axioms; and (iv) providing an empirical interpretation of the axiomatized theory. Suppes claimed that measurement theory relates to the fourth step and should show us how 'we may legitimately pass from the rough and ready region of qualitative, commonsense observations to the precise and metrical realm of systematic science' (p. 246).

At this point, Suppes explicitly asserted that there are 'various types of measurement', and noticed that in the literature there are 'several sets of axioms for measurement of different sorts' (p. 246). As examples, he listed the measurement axioms put forward by Hölder (1901/1996), Nagel (1931), von Neumann and Morgenstern (1944), Suppes

(1951), and Suppes and Winet (1953/1954). In a footnote, Suppes further noted that, from a mathematical viewpoint, the task of axiomatizing a given type of measurement is equivalent to 'the search for a representation theorem in the domain of real numbers, with the representation unique up to the appropriate transformations' (p. 246, footnote 9).

The above-quoted passages show that, by the end of 1953, Suppes had abandoned the classical understanding of measurement that had informed his 1951 article and endorsed the representational conception. Unlike Stevens, however, Suppes advocated an axiomatic approach, and more specifically a set-theoretical axiomatic approach, to the representational theory.

7. A coherent theory of measurement

A further step toward the elaboration of a systematic axiomatic theory of representational measurement can be found in the second installment of the Stanford Value Theory Project. This is the paper entitled 'Outlines of a Formal Theory of Value. I', which Suppes co-authored with Davidson and McKinsey. McKinsey had read an earlier and much shorter version of the paper in May 1953 at a seminar at the University of California at Los Angeles. After his death, Davidson and Suppes expanded and revised the work, which was eventually published in the April 1955 issue of *Philosophy of Science*.

In this article, Davidson et al. (1955, p. 141) put forward different sets of axioms identifying normative conditions for a 'rational preference pattern' in choice behavior. In particular, they claimed that a rational preference pattern must satisfy transitivity and, in support of this claim, they put forward the argument for which the article is usually cited in the economics literature, namely the so-called 'money pump argument.' Basically, Davidson, McKinsey, and Suppes showed that an individual with intransitive preferences – a hypothetical university professor they called Mr. S. – can be induced to pay money for nothing (pp. 145, 146).[12] For our purposes, however, the most important part of their article is the aside on measurement theory contained in Section 3.

In this section Davidson, McKinsey, and Suppes explicitly adopted the scale-of-measurement terminology and, without citing Stevens, they introduced a classification of measurement scales that closely resembles the one introduced by the Harvard psychologist in 1946. They identified, in order of increasing strength, the 'ordinal,' 'interval,' and 'ratio' scales, already discussed by Stevens, as well as the 'absolute scale,' which does not admit any arbitrary element and can be transformed only by the identity function $f(x) = x$. A magnitude measurable according to the absolute scale is probability.

Furthermore, just like Stevens, Davidson, McKinsey and Suppes criticized the traditional identification of measurement with classical, i.e. ratio, measurement, and noticed that such identification was still widespread in a number of philosophical treatises of their day. They argued that 'this ratio requirement is too rigid,' and that the erroneous identification of measurement with ratio measurement 'lies in the assumption that the only things which are measurable in a strong sense are […] magnitudes for which there exists a natural operation corresponding closely to the addition of numbers' (p. 151). This error also 'led to the erroneous view that no kind of measurement appropriate to physics is applicable to psychological phenomena' (p. 151, footnote 8).

Moving to the measurement of preferences, Davidson, McKinsey, and Suppes agreed that preferences 'cannot be measured in the sense of a ratio scale,' but added that this circumstance does not exclude 'the possibility [...] that preferences can be measured in the sense of an interval scale' (p. 151), i.e. using a cardinal utility function, which latter was the view they supported.

The aside on measurement concludes with a passage in which Davidson, McKinsey and Suppes defined the concept of 'coherent theory of measurement.' This concept expresses, succinctly but with great precision, the conception of measurement Suppes was going to articulate in his subsequent works:

> A coherent theory of measurement is given by specifying axiomatically conditions imposed on a structure of empirically realizable operations and relations. The theory is formally complete if it can be proved that any structure satisfying the axioms is isomorphic to a numerical structure of a given kind (p. 151).

8. Experimental utility measurement

Part of the Stanford Value Theory Project centered on an experiment aimed at measuring the utility of money of a number of individuals on the basis of their preferences between gambles where small amounts of real money were at stake. The experiment relied on an axiomatization of EUT elaborated for the occasion by Davidson and Suppes (1956) – in the third Stanford Value Theory Project paper – and generated cardinal measures of utility.[13] In a second phase of the experiment, these cardinal measures of utility were used to test the validity of EUT.

An earlier experiment to measure the utility of money within the EUT framework had been conducted between 1948 and 1949 by Frederick Mosteller, a Harvard statistician who, in the late 1940s, had become interested in experimental psychology, and Philip Nogee, then a Harvard PhD student in psychology (Mosteller & Nogee, 1951). Beginning in November 1953, Davidson and Suppes began thinking about an experiment that could overcome a number of limitations they saw in the Mosteller-Nogee design. However, neither Davidson nor Suppes had any previous experience in experimental investigation, and they therefore brought Sidney Siegel into the project. Siegel (1916–1961), then completing his PhD in psychology at Stanford, had begun his doctoral studies in 1951 at the age of 35, having previously taken a rather singular biographical and educational path (Engvall Siegel, 1964). In the doctoral dissertation he completed in fall 1953, Siegel presented a possible measure of authoritarianism based on experimental techniques (Siegel, 1954).

Davidson, Suppes, and Siegel conducted their experiment in spring 1954. They presented their experimental results in a Stanford Value Theory Project report published in August 1955 and then, two years later, in the book *Decision Making: An Experimental Approach* (1957). Like Mosteller and Nogee, Davidson, Suppes, and Siegel concluded that it is feasible to measure experimentally the utility of money in a cardinal way, and also that their experimental findings supported the validity of EUT. I have discussed in detail the design and findings of their experiment, as well as its relationship with the Mosteller-Nogee study, in another paper (Moscati, in press). Here, I would like to call attention to the measurement-theoretic view underlying the Davidson-Suppes-Siegel study.

At the beginning of the book, the role of the Davidson-Suppes axiomatization of EUT used in the experiment is presented in unmistakably representational terms:

> We require that the axioms [...] permit us to prove (a) that is possible to assign numbers to the elements of any set [...] in such a way as to preserve the structure imposed on such

sets by the axioms, and (b) any two assignments of numbers [...] are related by some specified group of transformations (Davidson et al., 1957, p. 6).

In particular, the authors specify that the axioms 'yield interval measurement of utility.' (p. 6). They also present the findings of the experiment using the scale-of-measurement terminology of the representational view:

> The chief experimental result may be interpreted as showing that for some individuals and under appropriate circumstances it is possible to measure utility in an interval scale. (p. 19)

The book was the last research item of the Stanford Value Theory Project to be published. As we have seen, between the beginning of the project in 1953 and the publication of its last item in 1957, Suppes' views on measurement changed significantly. He moved beyond the classical understanding of measurement that he initially reckoned on, definitely embraced the representational view, and envisaged, under the label of 'a coherent theory of measurement,' the project of a thoroughgoing axiomatization of the representational approach to measurement. His first decisive step toward the realization of this project is represented by a paper he co-authored with Dana Scott.

9. A conceptual framework for axiomatic measurement theory

Dana S. Scott (born 1932) studied mathematics and logic at the University of California at Berkeley, where he became a pupil of Alfred Tarski (Burdman Feferman and Ferferman 2004). Suppes had met Scott in 1952, when the latter was an undergraduate student in a course on the philosophy of science that Suppes taught at Berkeley (Suppes, 1979). After completing his BA in 1954, Scott moved to Princeton University for doctoral studies under Alonzo Church, another prominent logician, and received his PhD in 1958.

Scott and Suppes completed a first version of their joint paper, which is entitled 'Foundational Aspects of Theories of Measurement', in April 1957; the paper was later published in the June 1958 issue of the *Journal of Symbolic Logic*.[14] In the article, Scott and Suppes did not work out a systematic treatment of the axiomatic theory of measurement but rather delineated the conceptual framework in which such a treatment could be developed. Although this conceptual framework remained fundamentally set-theoretical in nature, it also incorporated some elements of the logic-based approach to axiomatization about which, as mentioned above, Suppes (1954) had expressed some skepticism. These logic-based elements can be explained by the fact that Suppes' co-author was a logician and that the article was published in a symbolic-logic journal.

Scott and Suppes (1958) grounded their conceptual framework in the notion of a *relational system* that Tarski (1954/1955) had recently introduced. A relational system $\mathfrak{A} = \langle A, R_1, \ldots, R_n \rangle$ is a set-theoretical structure in which A is a non-empty set of elements called the *domain* of $\mathfrak{A}$, and $R_1, \ldots, R_n$ are relations between one, two, or more elements of A (functions connecting elements of A can be conceived as relations). For instance, A_1 can be a set of sounds and R_1 the binary relation 'louder than' expressing the acoustic judgment of a given subject; then $\mathfrak{A}_1 = \langle A_1, R_1 \rangle$ is a relational system. Using the notion of relational system, the intuitive idea of isomorphism can be made precise. Two relational system $\mathfrak{A} = \langle A, R_1, \ldots, R_n \rangle$ and $\mathfrak{B} = \langle B, S_1, \ldots, S_n \rangle$ are said to be isomorphic if there exists a one-to-one function f from A onto B such that, for each relation R_i and for each sequence $\langle a_1, \ldots, a_m \rangle$ of elements of A, the relation R_i holds on these elements if and only if a relation S_i holds for the image of $\langle a_1, \ldots, a_m \rangle$ in B through f, that is, $R_i(a_1, \ldots, a_m)$ if and only if $S_i(f(a_1), \ldots, f(a_m))$.

A *numerical relational system* $\mathfrak{N} = \langle \mathbb{R}, N_1, \ldots, N_n \rangle$ is a system whose domain of elements is the set $\mathbb{R}$ of real numbers. A *numerical assignment* for a relation system $\mathfrak{A}$ with respect to a numerical relational system $\mathfrak{N}$ is a function f from A onto $\mathbb{R}$ such that $R_i(a_1, \ldots, a_m)$ if and only if $N_i(f(a_1), \ldots, f(a_m))$. The function f does not need to be one-to-one, for in many cases we may want to assign the same number to two distinct objects. If such a numerical function f exists, Scott and Suppes call the relation system $\mathfrak{A}$ *imbeddable* in $\mathfrak{N}$. Using a less esoteric terminology, we could say that the relation system $\mathfrak{A}$ is represented by the numerical relational system $\mathfrak{N}$.

After all these preliminaries, by the end of the first section of their paper Scott and Suppes (1958, p. 115) could finally define 'a theory of measurement' as a class K of isomorphic relational systems for which there exists 'a numerical relational system $\mathfrak{N}$ [...] such that all relational systems in K are [...] imbeddable in $\mathfrak{N}$.'

In the second section, Scott and Suppes investigated the conditions under which a theory of measurement for a given class of relational systems exists. In the 3 Section, they moved to the issue of axiomatizability. They called a theory of measurement *axiomatizable* if there exists 'a set of sentences of first-order logic (the axioms of the theory)', such that 'a relational system is in the theory if and only if the system satisfies all the sentences in the set' (p. 123).[15] Without entering here into technical details, we can say that Scott and Suppes showed that the existence and axiomatizability of a theory of measurement depend, among other things, on whether the domain of the relational system is finite or infinite, and on which type of numerical relations N_i are considered.

For our purposes, what is particularly important is that Scott and Suppes illustrated their new conceptual framework for measurement theory with examples taken from utility analysis. In these examples, the domain A of a relational system is constituted by a set of choice objects, and the relations $\langle R_1, \ldots, R_n \rangle$ on A are preference relations over these objects satisfying certain axioms. In particular, Scott and Suppes (pp. 118–122) considered preference axioms analogous to those used by Suppes and Winet (1955) in their utility-difference model, the axioms introduced by Luce (1956) in his model of semi-ordered preferences, as well as the axioms used in the probabilistic theory of choice, which was an approach to utility analysis quite fashionable in the second half of the 1950s.[16]

Given that Scott's background was in mathematics and logic, it seems fair to assume that these examples taken from utility analysis are due to Suppes. This circumstance reinforces the main point made in the present paper, namely that Suppes' early work in measurement theory was crucially influenced by his contemporaneous engagement with utility analysis.

10. Epilogue and summary

In their 1958 article, Scott and Suppes explained how certain traditional problems of measurement theory, namely those related to the assignment of numbers to objects, could be restated and clarified within the new conceptual framework they put forward. However, they barely discussed the problems related to the class of transformations the assigned numbers can be legitimately subjected to, and did not explain how these problems could be expressed within their new framework. Moreover, although Scott and Suppes illustrated their framework by examples taken from utility analysis, these illustrations were far from systematic. In particular, they did not explain how the theory for each of the four scales typically discussed in measurement analysis would look like in the new framework. In the following years, this work of clarification and systematization was undertaken by Suppes and Zinnes in the first chapter of the *Handbook of Mathematical Psychology* (1963), and finalized by Krantz, Luce, Suppes, and Tversky in the *Foundations of Measurement* (1971, 1989, 1990). A discussion of these developments is beyond the scope of the present paper. However, it is worth noting that both the Suppes-Zinnes chapter and the *Foundations of Measurement* adopt a set-theoretical rather than logical approach.

This paper has reconstructed the connections between the work Suppes did in utility theory between 1953 and 1957 within the Stanford Value project, and the evolution of his measurement theory from 1951 to 1958. The constant element in Suppes' approach to measurement theory was his steadfast reliance on the set-theoretical axiomatic method. What changed was his conception of what it means to measure a thing. Because his background was in philosophy, mathematics, and physics, Suppes in 1951 conformed to the classical conception of measurement dominant in these disciplines. But his subsequent involvement with psychology, economics, and the behavioral sciences in general helped him understand that the classical view was too narrow to account for the quantification practices used in these disciplines. Thus, he embraced the broader representational concept of measurement that had been expounded by Stevens in the 1940s. But while Stevens was not interested in giving the representational theory an axiomatic treatment, Suppes was. The first, decisive step in the realization of this ambitious project was the article Suppes co-authored with Scott in 1958.

In an autobiographical article, Suppes (1979) recalled that his views on measurement had its origins in the work he conducted within the Stanford Value Theory Project. Nevertheless, hitherto there has existed no systematic study integrating Suppes' memories with a detailed analysis of his early research in measurement theory and utility analysis. The present essay has filled this lacuna, and in doing so has showed that Suppes' superseding of the classical understanding of measurement, his endorsement of the representational view, and his conceiving of an axiomatic version of the latter were all driven by the research in utility analysis that he carried out within the Project.

Acknowledgements

I am grateful to Jean Baccelli, Simon Cook, Marco Dardi, John Davis, and Philippe Mongin for helpful comments on earlier versions of this paper. The usual disclaimer applies.

Disclosure statement

No potential conflict of interest was reported by the author.

Funding

This work was supported by Fondazione Cariplo and the European Society for the History of Economic Thought.

Notes

1. Since the early 1950s Milton Friedman and Savage (1952), and also other economists, had pointed out that from a strictly theoretical viewpoint EUT does not imply a return to cardinal utility (Moscati, 2016). Historically, however, this ordinal interpretation of EUT was not shared by all users of EUT, who included, besides economists, operation research scholars, philosophers, psychologists, and mathematicians (Erikson & others, 2013; Heukelom, 2014). In particular, in the works of Suppes, and notably in those he published between

1951 and 1958, I was not able to find any trace of the ordinal interpretation of EUT. For Suppes, the mathematical function featuring in the expected utility formula *was* a cardinal utility function. For a more extended discussion of Suppes' approach to cardinal utility, see Baccelli and Mongin (2016).

2. Suppes' seven axioms (1951, pp. 164, 165) are as follows: (1) $\leq$ is transitive; (2) $+$ is closed in the set of objects K; (3) $+$ satisfies the associative law; (4) if x, y and z are in K, and $x \leq y$, then $(x + z) \leq (y + z)$, i.e., 'adding' the same element does not alter order; (5) if x and y are in K, and not $x \leq y$, then there is a z in K such that $x \leq y + z$ and $y + z \leq x$, that is, any element x may be obtained by 'summing' two other elements y and z; 6: if x and y are in K, then not $x + y \leq x$, that is, 'sum' is greater than the 'summands'; 7: if x and y are in K and $x \leq y$, then there is a number n such that $y \leq nx$ (Archimedean property).

3. The other three scales are identified by the following classes of transformations. Nominal scale: transformations by any one-to-one function $f(x)$. Ordinal scale: transformations by monotonically increasing functions, i.e. by any $f(x)$ with positive first derivative f'. Ratio scale: proportional transformations by functions of the form $f(x) = \alpha x$, with $\alpha > 0$.

4. Stevens' non-axiomatic stance is related to his endorsement of the operational epistemology put forward by Bridgman (1927). On Stevens' operationalism and its relationship with his measurement theory, see Hardcastle (1995) and Michell (1999).

5. In his 1946 article, Stevens did not cite *Theory of Games*. However, in a footnote in a later paper, Stevens (1951, p. 23) acknowledged the similarity between his measurement theory and that of von Neumann and Morgenstern. In order to anticipate possible priority issues, Stevens claimed that he had presented his theory 'before the International Congress for the Unity of Science, September 1941.' I have found no evidence refuting this claim. Apparently, Stevens and von Neumann-Morgenstern arrived at similar theories of measurement in an independent way around the same time.

6. More on McKinsey's scientific contributions and personality in Davidson, Goheen, and Suppes (1954), Lepore (2004), and Burdman Feferman, and Feferman (2004). This last book is also a good reference for Tarski's work in logic.

7. On the reasons why in the 1950s the Ford Foundation and military agencies such as the Office of Naval Research were interested in funding research on decision-making, see Pooley and Solovey (2010), and Erikson and others (2013).

8. In 1957, Winet completed her PhD at Stanford under Suppes with a dissertation on *Interval Measurement of Subjective Magnitudes with Subliminal Differences* (Wood Winet Gerlach, 1957), a topic strictly related to that of the article co-authored with her advisor.

9. Alt's article had been published in German in the Austrian journal *Zeitschrift für Nationalökonomie*, which in 1936 was directed by Morgenstern. Although Morgenstern, Lange, and Samuelson were aware of its existence, Alt's article became known to a larger English-speaking public only after it was mentioned by Joseph Schumpeter in his *History of Economic Analysis* (Schumpeter, 1954, p. 1063). More on Alt, his axiomatization of cardinal utility, and the fortunes of his article in Moscati (2015).

10. Suppes and Winet's axioms are as follows. Axioms 1–4 require that both Q and R are complete and transitive. Axiom 5 imposes that only the 'extension' of the interval between two elements x and y matter, and not the relative order of x and y; thus interval (x,y) is equivalent to interval (y,x). Axiom 6 means that any interval (x,y) can be bisected, i.e. that for any two elements x and y there exists a midpoint element t such that interval (x,t) is equivalent to interval (t,y). Axiom 7 states that, if two elements x and y are indifferent, then one can be substituted for the other without modifying the order relationships among intervals: if xQy, yQx, and $(x,z)R(u,v)$, then $(y,z)R(u,v)$. Axiom 8 requires that, if y is between x and z, then the interval between x and y is smaller than the interval between x and z. Axiom 9 is an additivity assumption on R: if interval (x,y) is smaller than interval (u,w), and interval (y,z) is smaller than interval (w,v), then the 'sum' (x,z) of the two smaller intervals is smaller than the 'sum' (u,v) of the two larger intervals. Axiom 10 imposes a continuity property: if interval (x,y) is strictly smaller than interval (u,v), then there is an element t between u and v such that interval (x,y) is still not greater than interval (u,t). Axiom 11 is an Archimedean assumption; it fundamentally states that each interval can be expressed as the sum of a finite sequence of smaller, equivalent intervals.

11. Baccelli and Mongin (2016) discuss the problems associated with Suppes and Winet's focus on absolute rather than simple (i.e. algebraic) utility differences.

12. For an introduction to the money pump argument, see Anand (1993).
13. The Davidson-Suppes axiomatization has two main distinguishing features: (i) it is based on the subjective approach to probability and EUT pioneered by Frank Ramsey (1926/1950) and developed by Savage (1954), and (ii) it is 'finitistic,' in the sense that the set of alternatives over which the individual's preferences are defined is not infinite, as it is in the Ramsey-Savage framework, but finite. Suppes (1956) presented an alternative version of the Davidson-Suppes axiomatization of subjective EUT. Neither Davidson and Suppes (1956) nor Suppes (1956) addressed measurement issues in detail, and therefore these articles are of only modest relevance for the present paper. For a more extended discussion of Suppes' subjective version of EUT, see Baccelli and Mongin (2016).
14. In April 1957, Suppes also completed an introductory textbook on logic, which he dedicated to the memory of McKinsey (Suppes, 1957, p. v). The last chapter of the book is devoted to the set-theoretical foundations of the axiomatic method, while elsewhere in it Suppes briefly discusses measurement theory (pp. 265, 266). This discussion, however, does not add any new elements to the picture drawn so far.
15. First-order logic allows for quantification over objects. In particular, it admits the universal quantifier ∀ ('for every object') and the existential quantifier ∃ ('there exists an object'). However, first-order logic does not permit quantification over sets of objects ('for every set of objects'), for which second-order logic is required.
16. In order to account for situations in which an individual cannot discriminate between similar objects, Luce (1956) considered a generalization of standard utility theory in which the relation of strict preference between objects is transitive while the indifference relation is not. Such a preference structure is called a 'semiorder,' and Luce showed how to construct a utility function that assigns numbers to semi-ordered objects. In the probabilistic approach to choice, put forward by Marschak (1955), Quandt (1956) and other economists, it is assumed that when a subject chooses between the same pair of objects x and y more than once, because of judgment errors or other factors, sometimes he ranks x over y, and sometimes y over x. The subject is said to prefer x to y if the probability p_{xy} that he chooses x over y is at least 0.5, i.e., if $p_{xy} \geq 0.5$. If the probability p_{xy} is at least as large as the probability p_{zw} that he chooses z over w, i.e. if $p_{xy} \geq p_{zw}$, then the utility difference between x and y is considered to be at least as large as the utility difference between z and w. Under certain assumptions, probabilistic preferences can be represented by a cardinal utility function.

References

Alt, F. (1936/1971). On the measurability of utility. In J. S. Chipman (Ed.), *Preference, utility and demand* (pp. 424–431). New York, NY: Harcourt Brace Jovanovich.

Anand, P. (1993). The philosophy of intransitive preference. *Economic Journal, 103*, 337–346.

Baccelli, J., & Mongin, P. (2016). Choice-based cardinal utility. A tribute to Patrick Suppes. *Journal of Economic Methodology, 23*, this issue.

Blackwell, D., & Girshick, M. A. (1954). *Theory of games and statistical decisions*. New York, NY: Wiley.

Boumans, M. (2015). *Science outside the laboratory*. New York, NY: Oxford University Press.

Bridgman, P. W. (1927). *The logic of modern physics*. New York, NY: MacMillan.

Burdman Feferman, A., & Feferman, S. (2004). *Alfred Tarski. Life and logic*. New York, NY: Cambridge University Press.

Davidson, D., Goheen, J., & Suppes, P. (1954). J.C.C. McKinsey. *Proceedings and Addresses of the American Philosophical Association, 27*, 103–104.

Davidson, D., McKinsey, J. C. C., & Suppes, P. (1955). Outlines of a formal theory of value, I. *Philosophy of Science, 22*, 140–160.

Davidson, D., & Suppes, P. (1956). A finitistic axiomatization of subjective probability and utility. *Econometrica, 24*, 264–275.

Davidson, D., Suppes, P., & Siegel, S. (1957). *Decision making an experimental approach*. Stanford, CA: Stanford University Press.

Engvall Siegel, A. (1964). Sidney Siegel: A memoir. In S. Messick & A. H. Brayfield (Eds.), *Decision and choice. Contributions of Sidney Siegel* (pp. 1–24). New York, NY: McGraw-Hill.

Erikson, P. Klein, J. L., Daston, L., Lemov, R., Sturm, T., & Gordin, M. D. (2013). *How reason almost lost its mind*. Chicago, IL: University of Chicago Press.

Friedman, M., & Savage, L. J. (1952). The expected-utility hypothesis and the measurability of utility. *Journal of Political Economy, 60*, 463–474.

Frigerio, A., Giordani, A., & Mari, L. (2010). Outline of a general model of measurement. *Synthese, 175*, 123–149.

Hardcastle, G. L. (1995). S. S. Stevens and the origins of operationism. *Philosophy of Science, 62*, 404–424.

Heukelom, F. (2014). *Behavioral economics. A history*. New York, NY: Cambridge University Press.

Hilbert, D. (1899/1950). *The foundations of geometry*. La Salle, IL: Open Court.

Hölder, O. (1901/1996). The axioms of quantity and the theory of measurement, part I. *Journal of Mathematical Psychology, 40*, 235–252.

Isaac, J. (2013). Donald Davidson and the analytic revolution in American philosophy, 1940–1970. *Historical Journal, 56*, 757–779.

Krantz, D. H., Luce, R. D., Suppes, P., & Tversky, A. (1971). *Foundations of measurement*, Vol. 1. San Diego, CA: Academic Press.

Krantz, D. H., Luce, R. D., Suppes, P., & Tversky, A. (1989). *Foundations of measurement*, Vol. 2. San Diego, CA: Academic Press.

Krantz, D. H., Luce, R. D., Suppes, P., & Tversky, A. (1990). *Foundations of measurement*, Vol. 3. San Diego, CA: Academic Press.

Lange, O. (1934). The determinateness of the utility function. *Review of Economic Studies, 1*, 218–225.

Lepore, E. (2004). Interview with Donald Davidson. In D. Davidson (Ed.), *Problems of rationality* (pp. 231–266). Oxford: Oxford University Press.

Luce, R. D. (1956). Semiorders and a theory of utility discrimination. *Econometrica, 24*, 178–191.

Marschak, J. (1955). Norms and habits of decision making under certainty. In *Mathematical models of human behavior* (pp. 45–53). Stamford, CT: Dunlap and Associates.

McKinsey, J. C. C. (1952). *Introduction to the theory of games*. New York, NY: McGraw-Hill.

McKinsey, J. C. C., Sugar, A. C., & Suppes, P. (1953). Axiomatic foundations of classical particle mechanics. *Journal of Rational Mechanics and Analysis, 2*, 253–272.

McKinsey, J. C. C., & Suppes, P. (1953a). Transformations of systems of classical particle mechanics. *Journal of Rational Mechanics and Analysis, 3*, 273–289.

McKinsey, J. C. C., & Suppes, P. (1953b). Philosophy and the axiomatic foundations of physics. *Proceedings of the Eleventh International Congress of Philosophy, 6*, 49–54.

Michell, J. (1999). *Measurement in psychology*. Cambridge: Cambridge University Press.

Mongin, P. (2004). L'axiomatisation et les théories économiques [Axiomatization and economic theories]. *Revue économique, 54*, 99–138.

Mongin, P. (2009). Duhemian themes in expected utility theory. In A. Brenner & J. Gayon (Eds.), *French studies in the philosophy of science* (pp. 303–357). New York, NY: Springer.

Moscati, I. (2013a). Were Jevons, Menger, and Walras really cardinalists? On the notion of measurement in utility theory, psychology, mathematics, and other disciplines, 1870–1910. *History of Political Economy, 45*, 373–414.

Moscati, I. (2013b). How cardinal utility entered economic analysis, 1909–1944. *European Journal of the History of Economic Thought, 20*, 906–939.

Moscati, I. (2015). Austrian debates on utility measurement, from Menger to Hayek. In R. Leeson (Ed.), *Hayek: A collaborative biography, part IV* (pp. 137–179). New York, NY: Palgrave Macmillan.

Moscati, I. (2016). How economists came to accept expected utility theory: The case of Samuelson and Savage. *Journal of Economic Perspectives, 30*, 219–236.

Moscati, I. (in press). Measuring the economizing mind in the, 1940s and 1950s. The Mosteller–Nogee and Davidson–Suppes–Siegel experiments to measure the utility of money. *History of Political Economy, 48* (annual supplement).

Mosteller, F., & Nogee, P. (1951). An experimental measurement of utility. *Journal of Political Economy, 59*, 371–404.

Nagel, E. (1931). Measurement. *Erkenntnis, 2*, 313–333.

Nasar, S. (1998). *A beautiful mind*. New York, NY: Simon and Schuster.

Phelps Brown, E. H. (1934). Notes on the determinateness of the utility function, I. *Review of Economic Studies, 2*, 66–69.

Pooley, J., & Solovey, M. (2010). Marginal to the revolution: The curious relationship between economics and the behavioral sciences movement in mid-twentieth-century America. *History of Political Economy, 42* (annual supplement), 199–233.

Quandt, R. E. (1956). A probabilistic theory of consumer behavior. *Quarterly Journal of Economics, 70*, 507–536.

Ramsey, F. P. (1926/1950). Truth and probability. In R. B. Braithwaite (Ed.), *Foundations of mathematics and other logical essays* (pp. 156–198). New York, NY: Humanities Press.

Samuelson, P. A. (1938). The numerical representation of ordered classifications and the concept of utility. *Review of Economic Studies, 6*, 65–70.

Savage, L. J. (1954). *The foundations of statistics*. New York, NY: Dover.

Schumpeter, J. A. (1954). *History of economic analysis*. New York, NY: Oxford University Press.

Scott, D., & Suppes, P. (1958). Foundational aspects of theories of measurement. *Journal of Symbolic Logic, 23*, 113–128.

Siegel, S. (1954). Certain determinants and correlates of authoritarianism. *Genetic Psychology Monographs, 49*, 187–254.

Stevens, S. S. (1936). A scale for the measurement of a psychological magnitude; loudness. *Psychological Review, 43*, 405–416.

Stevens, S. S. (1946). On the theory of scales of measurement. *Science, 103*, 677–680.

Stevens, S. S. (1951). Mathematics, measurement and psychophysics. In S. S. Stevens (Ed.), *Handbook of experimental psychology* (pp. 1–49). New York, NY: Wiley.

Stevens, S. S., & Volkmann, J. (1940). The relation of pitch to frequency: A revised scale. *American Journal of Psychology, 53*, 329–353.

Suppes, P. (1951). A set of independent axioms for extensive quantities. *Portugaliae Mathematica, 10*, 163–172.

Suppes, P. (1954). Some remarks on problems and methods in the philosophy of science. *Philosophy of Science, 21*, 242–248.

Suppes, P. (1956). The role of subjective probability and utility in decision-making. In J. Neyman (Ed.), *Proceedings of the third Berkeley symposium on mathematical statistics and probability* (Vol. 5, pp. 61–73). Berkeley: University of California Press.

Suppes, P. (1957). *Introduction to logic*. New York, NY: Van Nostrand Reinhold.

Suppes, P. (1979). Self-profile. In R. J. Bogdan (Ed.), *Patrick Suppes* (pp. 3–56). Dordrecht: Reidel.

Suppes, P., & Winet, M. (1953/1954). An axiomatization of utility based on the notion of utility differences (abstract). *Bulletin of the American Mathematical Society, 60*, 81–82.

Suppes, P., & Winet, M. (1955). An axiomatization of utility based on the notion of utility differences. *Management Science, 1*, 259–270.

Suppes, P., & Zinnes, J. L. (1963). Basic measurement theory. In R. D. Luce, R. R. Bush, & E. Galanter (Eds.), *Handbook of mathematical psychology* (Vol. 3, pp. 1–76). New York, NY: Wiley.

Tarski, A. (1954/1955). Contributions to the theory of models. *Koninklijke Nederlandse Akademie van Wetenschappen*, Proceedings, series A, 57, 572–588, and 58, 56–64.

Von Neumann, J., & Morgenstern, O. (1944). *Theory of games and economic behavior*. Princeton, NJ: Princeton University Press.

Wood Winet Gerlach, M. (1957). *Interval measurement of subjective magnitudes with subliminal differences* (PhD dissertation). Stanford, CA: Department of Philosophy, Stanford University.

Choice-based cardinal utility: a tribute to Patrick Suppes

Jean Baccelli and Philippe Mongin

We reexamine some of the classic problems connected with the use of cardinal utility functions in decision theory, and discuss Patrick Suppes' contributions to this field in light of a reinterpretation we propose for these problems. We analytically decompose the doctrine of ordinalism, which only accepts ordinal utility functions, and distinguish between several doctrines of cardinalism, depending on what components of ordinalism they specifically reject. We identify Suppes' doctrine with the major deviation from ordinalism that conceives of utility functions as representing preference differences, while being nonetheless empirically related to choices. We highlight the originality, promises and limits of this choice-based cardinalism.

1. Introduction

This paper investigates the connection of choice data with cardinal utility functions. By the standards of today's microeconomics, the latter cannot rightfully represent the former. From the ordinal revolution of the first half of the twentieth century onwards, and despite the turn taken later by von Neumann and Morgenstern, neoclassical economists have been reluctant to allow into cardinal utility in economic theory. This reluctance is inseparable from the view, which spread out among them concurrently, that choices are the overarching kind of data to be considered. As microeconomics textbooks put it, 'cardinal utility [functions are not] needed to describe choice behavior' (Varian, 2005, p. 58), and if they nonetheless sometimes occur, they are 'simply convenient choices for a utility representation' (Mas-Colell, Whinston, & Green, 1995, p. 50). A pivotal claim, which is generally left implicit, underlies these familiar statements: *if choices are taken to constitute the empirical basis of economics, then cardinal utility loses its principled justifications*. Had today's neoclassical economists not adhered to this claim, they would have felt free to rely mainly or exclusively on choice data, and nonetheless leave more scope to cardinal utility than just what convenience reasons permit. However, by the current views, this sounds like an impossible theoretical combination.

A homage to Patrick Suppes provides a good occasion to examine the claim we have singled out.[1] In the post-war years, Suppes contributed to giving the nascent discipline of decision theory its operating standards, a collective undertaking in which many other prominent scholars were involved, were they among his close collaborators, like

Luce, or more loosely connected with him, like Marschak, Savage and other followers of von Neumann and Morgenstern. All these writers assigned to decision theory the task of proving *representation theorems*, i.e. theorems clarifying the equivalences holding between relational statements, typically interpreted as preference statements, and numerical statements, typically interpreted as utility statements, and all of them identified this proving task with an application of the axiomatic method as could be encountered elsewhere in logic, mathematics and science.[2] In this brilliant group of contributors, Suppes can be noted for two significant features. For one thing, he was generally concerned with the problem of measuring quantities, and as such conceived of the axiomatic exercise as a way to establish specific forms of measurement. In his quest for the most precise forms, he was led to emphasize cardinal representations as a suitable objective for his theorems. For another thing, being an empiricist philosopher and scientist, he took choices to be the privileged, if not unique, source of data the axiomatic exercise should pay attention to. In effect, without saying so much, *Suppes was running against the ordinalist tide of neoclassical economics*. We offer this not as a historical statement, but as a reinterpretation of his work, since he was neither initially trained nor primarily interested in economics as such (see his enlightening 1979 'Self-Profile', from which economics is almost absent).

In the first part of the paper, we give more flesh to the ordinalist tenets sketched at the beginning of this introduction; once again, we propose a conceptual reconstruction, and leave for others the full history of the matter. What we mean is to set a clear negative benchmark against which fruitful connections between choice and cardinal utility can be discussed. In the second part, we single out some of Suppes' contributions to the theory of cardinal representations, pertaining, respectively, to (i) choice under uncertainty, (ii) stochastic choice and (iii) choice under certainty. The third part elaborates on the conflict between these contributions and the ordinalist tenets of the first part. We highlight Suppes' suggestions on (iii), which in our view contains valuable advances. Extracting a general take-away message from his work, we end up cautiously defending the possibility of choice-based cardinal utility representations.

2. Ordinalism and its dissenters

Any discussion of the ordinalist tenets should begin with the celebrated discovery made by neoclassical writers at the dawn of the twentieth century. To recover the essentials of demand theory, it proved unnecessary to endow the individual consumer with a 'numerical' or 'measurable' utility function over the set of commodity baskets. A utility function that merely indicates the consumer's preference ordering over these baskets proves sufficient to deliver what can be salvaged from the old law of demand and related propositions. Before this major discovery, neoclassicals had developed demand theory from the law of decreasing marginal utilities or other assumptions that can be stated only if the utility function makes definite numerical sense. The standard account singles out Pareto (1909) for replacing this thick apparatus by a thinner one, and his followers like Slutsky (1915), Hicks and Allen (1934) and Hicks (1939) for bringing this replacement programme to completion. In this revised form of neoclassicism, utility functions would have to be *ordinal*, in the sense of being *unique up to any increasing transformation*. Henceforth, when we write that a utility function is 'ordinal', we refer to this definition. It appears to have stabilized before than the definition of a cardinal utility function did. Even relatively late in the twentieth century, neoclassical writers often adopted different words and different ideas to capture the more-than-ordinal features of a utility function.

They said not only 'cardinal', but also 'numerical', 'measurable' and 'quantitative', being quite vague – and no doubt disagreeing between themselves – on the kind of mathematical uniqueness they had in view for the utility function.[3]

As Hicks (1939, p. 18) writes,

> we have now to inquire whether a full theory of consumer's demand (...) cannot be built up from the assumption of a *scale of preference*. In constructing such a theory it will be necessary every time to reject any concept which is at all dependent on quantitative utility, so that it cannot be derived from the indifference map alone.

Beside testifying to the vagueness of ideas concerning 'quantitative utility', this comment is instructive in the following way: while Hicks means his explication to restrict the utility concept, it also turns out to restrict the preference concept. Preference is taken here to be a mere disposition to *rank* the objects of interest (or to classify them as being indifferent, which we include in our notion of a ranking). As Hicks goes on, 'we start off from the indifference map alone; nothing more can be allowed'. Among other things, this implies that unlike in some earlier approaches, there will be no room in the new theory for comparisons of the type '*i* prefers more intensely hot chocolate to coffee, than he prefers tea to herbal tea'. Such comparisons are undefined because they do something else than ranking options. Samuelson's *Foundations* (1947) exemplifies the glide, which we emphasize here, from the claim that utility is exclusively ordinal to the claim that preference also is.[4] The Paretians never made this claim explicitly, so it remains unclear whether they would have defended it as a semantic truth about the word 'preference', or as a technical restriction, which would be imposed for theoretical or other strategic purposes.

In whichever interpretation one takes, this slimmering of the preference concept was linked to a novel emphasis on choices as the appropriate basis for demand theory. In the *Manual*, Pareto himself had promoted his ordinal utility analysis by arguing not only that it was logically sufficient for demand theory, but also that it made this theory more empirical, hence – in his positivistic conception – more scientific. Allegedly, this upgrading of the theory followed because the consumers' *choices* were the new primitives (see, e.g. 1909, III, 36bis). To reconcile Pareto's claim on choices with the one made later by Hicks, to the effect that *preferences* are the primitives, one must assume that the psychological data of preferences can be expressed sufficiently well by the external facts of choice. One way or another, this further reductive assumption underlay all the Paretians' work even before Samuelson, starting with his 1938 paper, gave it the famous twist of 'revealed preference'. Without elaborating here on individual positions, we wish to emphasize that all Paretians supposed a close affinity between preferences and choices, and this could only reinforce their slim conception of preferences. Indeed, to choose among options is to select some and leave others aside; from barely observing this activity, it seems easy to infer a preference understood as a ranking of options, and impossible to infer anything like a preference intensity.

Our detour by demand theory can be excused by the historical fact that it defined a benchmark for the analysis of economic decision-making in general. This benchmark is what we are interested in here. We call it *ordinalism* and summarize it by three reductive tenets: (1) utility functions are merely a formal representation of preferences, (2) preferences are merely a disposition to order the possible options, (3) choices merely inform the observer on how preferences order options. We take (2) as denying that a subject compares preference differences in the same structured way as he does preference levels – in other words, as denying that the relation 'I prefer more *w* to *x* than I

34

do y to z' defines an ordering. If (2) holds, (3) automatically does, but if (2) does not hold, (3) may or may not hold. That is, if preferences have more than the ordering-of-options property, it may or may not be the case that choices inform the observer on this extra content. The possibility of either accepting or rejecting (3) when one rejects (2) is essential to our reconstruction.

It follows from (1) and (2) together that utility functions can only be ordinal. A more traditional account of ordinalist ideas would have extracted this last claim and commented on it as follows: utility functions can only be ordinal *because* they merely represent preferences. We object to this account on the ground that it takes for granted the ordinalist conception of preferences as being mere rankings, and thus gives the false impression that the ordinal property of utility functions directly follows from their representational property. This virtually reduces ordinalism to claim (1) as if there were nothing more to ordinalism. By making the conception of preferences the object of a separate commitment, we make it clear that two separate claims underlie the uniqueness property of utility functions. Thus, our framework allows for the logical possibility that a utility function be *merely representational and nonetheless represent preference differences*, satisfying (1) but violating (2), and this will indeed be the conception we attribute to Suppes. A different objection to the more standard accounts, we think that ordinalism should be discussed not only in terms of the preference but also in terms of the choice concept, although one must be careful here not to confuse ordinalism with the revealed preference methodology (the latter being only a particular development of the former).

The present account can be compared with Mongin and d'Aspremont's briefer comments (Mongin & d'Aspremont, 1998, pp. 385–386), which emphasize (2) as a separate claim, and the addition made by Bruni and Guala (2001, p. 24). The last authors rightly emphasize that ordinalists limited the role of psychological assumptions in economics. This feature actually derives from the present list as follows: claim (1) excludes that utility has a psychological basis in the psychological feeling of subjective satisfaction (as in most classical and early neoclassical views), claim (2) excludes part of the psychological content one may associate with the concept of preference and claim (3) minimizes the psychological content of choice information.[5]

To further illustrate the logical content of the three tenets, and also to prepare the upcoming comparison with Suppes, we consider a historical departure from (2) that predated his work and to some extent influenced it. In an allusive passage of the *Manual* (1909, IV, §32), Pareto had claimed that, when faced with four commodity baskets w, x, y, z, the consumer can know whether he is more satisfied passing from x to w, or passing from z to y. This is a striking early occurrence of the claim that comparisons can be made not only between levels of satisfaction but also between differences in these levels. However, as could be expected from the founder of ordinalism, Pareto had considered such comparisons only to exclude them; for him, they lacked sufficient 'precision' to be subjected to a scientific inquiry. But Lange (1934) spotted the curious passage and tried to develop it in a positive direction. He claimed that a subject comparing Paretian 'transitions' could be endowed with a 'cardinal' utility function. Lange's sketch of proof was unsound, as others – prominently the mathematician Alt (1936–1971) – were soon to demonstrate. But he had launched a line of research that implicitly rejected the ordinalist claim (2). Lange's analysis unfolded at the level of utility representations alone, and thus remained equivocal, but Alt made a step towards the rejection of (2) by introducing a *quaternary ordering* on the options, i.e. an ordering that compares *pairs* of options (w, x) and (y, z). Putting axioms on this new primitive term, he obtained a utility function on the options with a relevant uniqueness property, thus proving one of the first representation theorems ever, and more specifically opening the way to Suppes' work along the same line. To the extent that Alt's ordering can be interpreted as a *preference* ordering, he can be said to have opposed (2) and thus shaken ordinalism at the peak of its theoretical success.

Without mentioning Pareto's passage, and probably without being aware of it, Frisch (1926, 1932) had already formalized comparisons of 'displacements' in the commodity space by a quaternary relation. However, this is a formalization without a proper axiomatization, and in point of fact, only a brief detour in two pieces that are primarily concerned with the empirical measurement of marginal utility. We mention Frisch nonetheless because Suppes refers to Frisch, though not to Alt, whose more significant contribution became recognized only belatedly.[6]

The programme initiated by Lange leaves two ordinalist tenets in place. Consistently with (1), it takes utility to have no meaning per se, but only to serve as a representation device, and consistently with (3), it limits choices to providing basic ranking information. This last point calls for more detail. Lange and followers tended to take *introspection* to be the single source of the quaternary comparisons, and we interpret this restrictive position as being dictated by continuing adherence to (3). A comment that Allen published on Lange's work makes this connection of ideas entirely explicit:

> It has been suggested that a second basic assumption can be added to the one already made [on the existence of a preference ranking of alternatives]. This assumption refers to changes in the 'intensity' of the preferences expressed by the individual. It implies, in short, that *the individual can distinguish increments of preference and that he can order these increments in the same way as the preferences themselves*. Here we are dealing with something quite new. The assumption cannot be expressed in terms of the individual's acts of choice; *it can only be supported by introspection* into one's own experience or by questioning others about their experiences. (Allen, 1935, p. 155, our emphasis)

Notice that Allen's lines also testify to the fact that Lange's readers thought of quaternary comparisons as being preference comparisons. Once a classic, Allen's (1956, pp. 669–676) text on mathematical economics discusses 'ordinal' versus 'measurable' utility along the same lines as his briefer comment on Lange.

A different argument on ordinalism became available when von Neumann and Morgenstern (1947, Appendix), and more clearly their followers, connected the time-honoured expected utility (EU) formula with a preference ordering over lotteries. This collective work, which Suppes witnessed when it was still in progress, converged to the classic theorem stating that, given relevant axiomatic conditions, the ordering has a representation in terms of this EU formula. The uniqueness clause of the theorem seemed to endow the utility function in this formula with a numerical ('measurable') property, and this raised puzzlement among post-war economists, who, by then, had been heavily exposed to ordinalist ideas. An intricate and profuse discussion resulted among them. Some claimed that von Neumann and Morgenstern (VNM) had rehabilitated the 'cardinal utility' of the classical and early neoclassicals, others, that this was not the case but they had nonetheless obtained a 'cardinal utility' function of their own, and still others, that neither was the case and that their EU representation was in fact ordinal. Although this would contextualize Suppes' work more fully, it goes beyond the scope of this paper to review the post-war debate on 'the cardinal utility which is ordinal', to use Baumol's (1958) striking words, and we refer the reader to the existing historical work in Fishburn (1989) and Moscati (2013a, 2016a). But we will briefly indicate the two key technical factors of this debate, which, respectively, concern the uniqueness property of the VNM utility function and its ability to induce a measurement of preference differences.

Let us then take a closer look at the VNM representation theorem. Its conclusion actually decomposes into an existence and a uniqueness part. According to the former, there exists a utility function u on the final outcomes X such that the preference ordering of two lotteries P and Q coincides with the comparison made between the expected utility values $E_P u$ and $E_Q u$ of these two lotteries. Formally, if one denotes by R the primitive weak preference ordering:

$$PRQ \text{ if and only if } E_P u \geq E_Q u.$$

According to the latter, uniqueness part, the function u is unique up to a positive affine transformation (PAT)[7] *in this representation*. Formally, if u' is another utility function on X, the following equivalence holds:

$$PRQ \text{ if and only if } E_P u' \geq E_Q u'$$

if and only if u' is a PAT of u.

A simple argument shows that the italicized clause *in this representation* cannot be removed. Since the VNM axiomatization assumes no more than a preference ordering on lotteries, it follows that the $E_P u$ representation is in fact ordinal, i.e. unique up to any increasing transformation φ. For instance, $(E_P u)^2$ or $\exp(E_P u)$ are as admissible representations of the preferences over lotteries as is $E_P u$. This observation readily entails that there is no way of reinforcing the uniqueness conclusion for u. For suppose that u were unique to PAT unrestrictedly; then the representation $E_P u$ would be unique up to PAT, and not up to any increasing transformation as was just said.

This discussion suggests introducing two notions of a cardinal utility function for the remainder of the paper. Let us say that a utility function on some set of options is *absolutely* cardinal if it is unique up to PAT, and that it is *relatively* cardinal if it is unique up to PAT for a given format of representation, such as the EU format here. We will see that this contrast applies broadly. As far as VNM theory is concerned, a good deal of the post-war debate can be explained by the fact that many protagonists missed the contrast entirely. Those who claimed that VNM had rehabilitated the 'cardinal utility' of the classical and early neoclassicals were off the mark, since they ignored the new feature of VNM utility being obtained by a representation theorem, but even those who claimed that VNM had obtained a 'cardinal utility' function of their own were not always correct, since some wrongly believed that the u of the representation theorem was *absolutely* cardinal. And those who claimed that this u was ordinal missed the important point that a *relatively* cardinal utility obeys a stronger uniqueness restriction than an arbitrary ordinal utility function.

The other key factor of the controversy has to do with the following argument, which was often discussed in the controversy (see a classic occurrence in Luce & Raiffa, 1957, pp. 31–34). Once the EU representation is obtained from the existence conclusion of the VNM theorem, a utility difference formalism becomes readily available. Take two equiprobable lotteries between w and x, and between y and z, respectively, and suppose that the preference ordering puts the first strictly above the second. Then,

$$\frac{1}{2}u(w) + \frac{1}{2}u(z) > \frac{1}{2}u(y) + \frac{1}{2}u(x),$$

which is trivially equivalent to:

$$u(w) - u(x) > u(y) - u(z).$$

Many participants to the debate took the comparisons of *utility* differences thus obtained to represent corresponding *preference* differences; in the particular instance, they would have concluded that the subject prefers w to x more than he prefers y to z. This understanding of VNM utility differences points towards the alternative definition of a cardinal utility function as being one that can represent not only preference levels, but also preference differences, and this alternative definition was indeed present in the debate, while being unclearly related to the formal definitions of the previous paragraph. This compounded the confusion already created by the poor understanding of the formal definitions. We refrain from saying more on VNM utility differences at the present stage, since this issue will come out again when we discuss Suppes in Section 4.

As a summary on the VNM theorem, we compare it with the three ordinalist tenets. It gives a purely representational sense to the EU formula, thus supporting (1). Whether it also supports (2) is a complex issue, depending on how one views the utility difference argument of last paragraph. If one rejects (2) on the ground that VNM utility can measure preference differences, it seems obvious to reject (3), since choices among lotteries, in the plain sense of what counts as a choice, become a source of information on preference differences. The position we will attribute to Suppes concerning EU representations (more generally than the VNM representation) will consist of this twin rejection of (2) and (3). We now move to a description (Section 3) and an assessment (Section 4) of his contributions.

3 Suppes on utility differences

Suppes' decision-theoretic contributions respond to a unifying concern for scientific measurement. In a sequel of papers and books that culminated with the famous series of *The Foundations of Measurement* (starting in 1971), coauthored with Krantz, Luce and Tversky, he investigated various forms of measurement of empirical properties, and fitted them in a unified mathematical framework that permitted defining and comparing them rigorously. When he tackled decision-theoretic issues in separate pieces of research, he always emphasized that they entered the measurement framework as particular cases, and thus illustrated its heuristic fecundity.

This approach has some noticeable consequences. First of all, unlike many positivist philosophers and scientists, Suppes does not draw a sharp line between physical and psychological properties. What matters to him is whether or not they are empirical properties, and in case they are, what kind of measurement they are amenable to. With this open mind, when he discusses decision-theoretic issues, he does not discard introspection as a possible source of information and contents himself with the claim that choices are a better source. As one of his leading papers goes, 'many areas of economic and modern statistical theory do not warrant a behavioristic analysis of utility. In these domains there seems little reason to be ashamed of direct appeals to introspection' (Suppes & Winet, 1955, p. 261). In the same vein, Luce and Suppes

(1965, p. 273) write that introspection has been 'unduly depreciated in some of the modern literature on choice behavior'. Suppes' position is not fully explicit, but it seems to rely on the view that introspection provides empirical data no less than choices, and if choice data are altogether preferable, this is only because they support more secure forms of measurement.[8]

Second, Suppes practices the method of representation theorems to clarify measurement possibilities. In decision theory, this leads him to be critical of the VNM and Savage axiom systems, which he complains assume unrealistically large sets of options and preferences comparisons. His favourite manner involves taking a finite set of options and a subclass of the logically possible comparisons, even if this economy must be achieved at the expense of the elegance and generality of the representation theorems. When he cannot impose finiteness, he tries at least to avoid topological or measure-theoretic assumptions on the set of options; typically, instead of such assumptions, he introduces 'solvability conditions' among his axioms.

Third, the representation theorems that Suppes wishes for decision theory should deliver a utility difference representation (this will automatically entail a utility-level representation as a particular case). This search for a precise form of utility function does not reflect a predetermined conception of preference and choice but rather a scientific hope: to count as an empirical science, decision theory must be able at least sometimes to reach this stage of measurement, and carefully designing the observational or experimental design could perhaps bring about this result. With these general comments in place, we now sketch Suppes' contributions, using his own terms as much as possible. We will not emphasize the uniqueness problem of utility representations in the present section. This, along with other substantial comments, will be reserved for Section 4.

As Suppes and Winet (1955, p. 259) put at the outset, they are concerned with 'reviving the notion of utility differences' and believe they can do so by proving representations theorems that apply to several choice contexts at once. The authors mentioned *choice under uncertainty* and *choice under certainty*, and with the benefit of hindsight, we can add *stochastic choice*, which attracted Suppes' later interest. Still following Suppes and Winet, we distinguish two steps in this revival programme. Given a domain X and a quaternary relation $\succcurlyeq$ defined on X, the first, mathematical step is to subject the relational statements $wx \succcurlyeq yz$ to axiomatic conditions that will entail a representation in terms of utility differences, namely,

$$(*) \quad wx \succcurlyeq yz \text{ if and only if } u(w) - u(x) \geq u(y) - u(z),$$

for some u on X with a relevant uniqueness property. For this statement of the mathematical problem, Suppes and Winet are indebted to the authors discussed in last section – they cite both Frisch and Lange, although not Alt, who was not yet known. The second, this time informal step, is to check that the domain X and the axiomatic conditions on $\succcurlyeq$ are appropriate, given the interpretations for $\succcurlyeq$ provided by the above contexts. At this semantic level, Suppes and Winet depart from Frisch, Lange and Alt, since these predecessors had considered only one context, i.e. choice under certainty.

A preliminary comment is in order. The paper with Winet actually sets out to axiomatize an *absolute difference* representation, i.e.

$$(**) \quad wx \succcurlyeq yz \text{ if and only if } |u(w) - u(x)| \geq |u(y) - u(z)|.$$

39

It is however the *algebraic difference* representation (*) that Suppes' revival programme is concerned with. We find it slightly embarrassing that the same paper contains both the clearest statement of this programme and an unrepresentative implementation of it. We will leave aside (**) until the end of Section 4, where we argue in effect that Suppes should have axiomatized (*) rather then (**).

(i) *Choice under uncertainty.* This choice context is only briefly mentioned in the paper with Winet, but Suppes will return to it thoroughly later. If probabilities were given, Suppes would simply repeat the argument discussed in last section, and take $wx \succcurlyeq yz$ to hold if the subject weakly prefers an equiprobable lottery on w and z to another equiprobable lottery on y and x. Assuming the VNM theorem to hold, this would deliver the following equivalence:

$$wx \succcurlyeq yz \text{ if and only if } \frac{1}{2}u(w) + \frac{1}{2}u(z) \geq \frac{1}{2}u(y) + \frac{1}{2}u(x),$$

However, Suppes argues that the risk approach makes empirical sense only if 'psychological probabilities are identical with the (...) objective' ones, a very dubious assumption in his view.[9] In a deep and novel insight at this formative stage of decision theory, Suppes realizes that subjective probabilities are more fundamental than lotteries and VNM theory is in fact incomplete, since it takes probabilities as given only by mathematical convention. In today's textbook terminology, Suppes subordinates the theory of risk to that of uncertainty. This is also Savage's (1972/1954) insight and we will leave it for historians to explain what the respective influences were.

Moving now to the more appropriate uncertainty context, we denote by wA^*z (resp. yA^*x) the prospect of w (resp. y) obtaining if A^* occurs and z (resp. x) obtaining otherwise. According to Suppes' definition, $wx \succcurlyeq yz$ holds if the subject prefers wA^*z to yA^*x, with the event A^* being such that for all $x', y', x'A^*y' : y'A^*x'$. In the first sketch ever made of an axiomatization of subjective probabilities, Ramsey (1926, in 1931, p. 177) had singled out events like A^*, calling them 'ethically neutral' (a strange denomination); in words, A^* is such that a subject faced with two consequences x' and y' is equally willing to see x' realized on A^* and y' on its complementary, or to see y' realized on A^* and x' on its complementary. When Ramsey's axiomatic exercise is properly completed, a subjective expected utility (SEU) representation emerges and the ethically neutral event A^* receives probability 1/2, so that the prospects wA^*z and yA^*x can occupy the role of the two equiprobable lotteries of VNM theory, and the equivalence above holds, though with a more satisfactory interpretation of the equal probability values. A utility difference representation as in (*) follows from the equivalence. Two papers by Davidson and Suppes (1956) and Suppes (1956) implement the strategy of this paragraph, while for the first time bringing Ramsey's ideas to the stage of sharp representation theorems.[10]

We have stressed that Suppes' axiomatic method embodies strong empirical concerns, and this is reflected in Davidson and Suppes (1956) by two departures from Ramsey's implicitly unrestricted framework.[11] The set X of consequences is taken to be finite, and the axioms are so devised that once the SEU representation obtains, the consequences have *equally spaced utility values* and combine in the EU formula with only a *finite number of subjective probability values.* Moreover, the set of two-consequence prospects wA^*z is limited to *genuinely uncertain ones*, i.e. it excludes wA^*w (the certainty of w), which is justified by another empirical concern. Davidson and Suppes worry that if sure prospects enter the comparisons, they may introduce the distorting influence of what they call the 'utility of gambling'.[12] Lastly, unlike Ramsey, Davidson and Suppes restrict their axioms to *the indifference part* of the preference ordering on prospects, i.e. in statements of the form $wAz \sim yAx$, as against those representing the preference ordering in general, $wAz \succcurlyeq yAx$. In view of all these restrictions, their representation theorem can only be much weaker than those of Ramsey and (blurring the distinction between risk and uncertainty) VNM, but they fully endorse this implication: 'the relative weakness of the present theory is the price to be paid for making it more behavioristic' (1956, p. 26).

In Suppes' mind, an experimental stage had to follow these axiomatic preliminaries, and it took place in a separate work coauthored with an experimental psychologist (Davidson, Suppes, & Siegel, 1957). Suppes and his collaborators tried there to identify an event that would be 'ethically neutral' across the pool of subjects. This proved to be more challenging than expected, because the subjects appeared to express preferences over the events that a fair coin lands heads rather tails, or that a fair dice rolls to an odd number rather than an even one. The experimenters adopted a dice with either of two meaningless syllables, 'ZEJ' and 'ZOJ', engraved on each of the six sides, and thus eventually generated what appeared to them to be an 'ethically neutral' event A^*. From there, they proceeded to elicit utility differences by taking consequences to be small amounts of money (ranging over cents), both positive and negative. Whenever possible, utility functions were derived from these data. In principle, an empirical verdict on SEU theory should have ensued, but the data were in fact inconclusive, as Suppes came later to recognize.[13] When revisiting these experimental efforts, Luce (1979, p. 102) will also have to conclude that, careful as they were, 'they did not lead to a clear decision as to the adequacy of the expected-utility property'.

(ii) *Stochastic choice.* For good historical reasons, this choice context was not mentioned in Suppes and Winet, but once stochastic choice theory took off, Suppes developed an interest in the utility difference representations this theory delivers, so we have included it into his revival programme. (See the supporting comment in Suppes & Zinnes, 1963, p. 38.) Here $wx \succcurlyeq yz$ holds in terms of a comparison between the subject's choice probabilities. Formally,

$$wx \succcurlyeq yz \text{ if and only if } p(w,x) \geq p(y,z),$$

where $p(w, x)$ and $p(y, z)$ are the probabilities that the subject chooses w over x and that he chooses y over z, given the respective menus of options $\{w,x\}, \{y,z\} \subseteq X$. Relevant axiomatizations of $\succcurlyeq$ ensure that there exists a utility function u on X such that

$$p(w,x) \geq p(y,z) \text{ if and only if } u(w) - u(x) \geq u(y) - u(z).$$

Thus, as Luce and Suppes (1965, p. 334) mention, stochastic choice theory in axiomatic form provides another road to (*). Since the original papers by Davidson and Marschak (1959) and Block and Marschak (1960), this theory has received at least two possible interpretations. For both Suppes and Luce, the probabilities are choice frequencies when the choice task is repeated and the source of randomness lies in the choice itself, as against its psychological determining factors (among which the preferences). The alternative interpretation locates randomness in these determining factors themselves.[14]

Suppes witnessed the birth of the stochastic choice literature and observed its development carefully (the review in Luce & Suppes, 1965; Section 5, is still used as a reference today). He also contributed to it with two novel representation theorems (Suppes, 1961). They were part of a larger, now little-known project, the originality of which was that it did not take choice probabilities as given, but derived them in a supposedly rigorous 'behavioristic' fashion. The probabilities were the asymptotic result of a learning process, which consisted of the three stages of stimulus sampling, response conditioning and reinforcement. This work was also the occasion of sketching a 'dynamic theory of (...) the acquisition of a particular set of beliefs or values', which could override the 'static' character of standard representation theorems (1961, p. 186).

(iii) *Choice under certainty*. This is the other choice context that Suppes and Winet mention and it is the specific object of their axiomatic work. They illustrate it by three concrete variants, each of which represents a step towards experimentation. The first hinges on the subject's willingness to pay for exchanging options, and it is curiously reminiscent of the 'money pump argument' for the transitivity of preference that Davidson, McKinsey, and Suppes (1955, p. 146) introduced in the same year. This takes $wx \succcurlyeq yz$ to hold if the subject, when endowed with both x and z, is willing to pay at least as much to replace x by w as he is to replace z by y.[15] A closely related variant exploits the subject's willingness to work, with $wx \succcurlyeq yz$ holding if the subject, when endowed with both x and z, is ready to work at least as much to replace x by w as he is to replace z by y. As Suppes and Winet (1955, p. 260) observe, the common idea behind these two examples is that a monotonic variation in some agreed on quantity permits measuring utility differences, thus opening another road to (*). Without the word and without the historical reference, the third variant leads us back to Paretian 'transitions', i.e. $wx \succcurlyeq yz$ holds if, when endowed with both x and z, the subject is either more willing to exchange x for w than z for y, or indifferent between the two exchanges. By axiomatizing $\succcurlyeq$ appropriately, one gets the utility difference representation (*), with u on X satisfying a relevant uniqueness property. Because Suppes and Winet derived an absolute difference representation, proper axiomatizations of $\succcurlyeq$ conforming to the third variant needed to await Suppes' later work, e.g. in Krantz, Luce, Suppes, and Tversky (1971, p. 147; see also the restatement in Köbberling, 2006, p. 381).

Each of the suggested variants has its theoretical problems. As Luce and Suppes (1965, pp. 273–275) will recognize when revisiting them, the first two resort to a quantity that does not belong to the initial set of options. One may respond to this by redefining this set, but then the objection rebounds, since the subject's preference over the new options must be *separable*, and this is a substantial assumption to make.[16] That is, with options now defined as (x, m), where m is, say, a quantity of money, the subject must rank the m component always in the same way regardless of the value taken by the x component. This assumption may or may not be appropriate, given the objects represented by x. Now, the proposed scheme needs $\succcurlyeq$ also to be continuous; otherwise the subject could not determine what money amount m' makes the option (y, m') indifferent with (x, m), given two distinct x and y. Continuity is a significant assumption to make when the options are multidimensional.

The Paretian 'transitions' variant can eschew the separability and continuity problems above, but raises other queries. We may discard the objection that to assume that the subject initially has both x and z violates the principle that options should be *alternatives*, i.e. mutually exclusive objects, for it is enough to redefine them as being pairs (x, z) and think of the comparisons as being made on such pairs.[17] More importantly, it is not said whether the scheme applies unrestrictedly or only in those cases in which the subject either prefers w to x or prefers y to z. In the latter interpretation, the subject will always compare the status quo with a change for the better, and thus be faced with a genuine choice problem, but only nonnegative utility differences can be measured in this way. In the former interpretation, the subject will also compare the status quo with changes for the worse, and this permits measuring negative utility differences, but the meaning in terms of choices is not so clear. Indeed, the subject must be *forced* to decide between the two evils, and only an experimental context can create the conditions for a forced exchange to take place, whereas choices in the other case could in principle be observed non-experimentally. All in all, the information carried by such a decision seems to be less secure than that carried by choices in the other case.

Suppes and Winet (1955, p. 260) illustrate their use of 'transitions' by imagining a housewife faced with a pair of appliances, say a toaster and a waxer, and then confronted with the 'choice of trading the toaster for waffle iron, or the waxer for the blender'. From the corresponding passage, we conclude that Suppes envisaged changes for the worse as well as for the better.[18]

Suppes' writings contains regrettably little on context (iii). The article with Luce has the following comment: 'Unfortunately, we know of no experiments that have attempted to apply either of these methods to the measurement of utility differences' (1965, p. 274). This in particular indicates that he never set himself the task of experimenting with the three concrete variants of (iii). Perhaps he found work along this line too novel and difficult, perhaps he did not value it so much as he did work on (i) and (ii), which connected better with his broader theoretical projects.

We now clarify the extent to which Suppes' contributions conflict with ordinalism and try to decide whether they bring out cogent arguments against it.

4. Suppes and ordinalism

Suppes claimed to be a philosopher and a social scientist, not an economist. As such, he had no theoretical stake with debasing ordinalism, but he was well aware that his approach to cardinal utility went against orthodox economic theory. For instance, Luce and Suppes (1965, p. 273) write: 'if we speak of the utility difference, or the difference in preference, between pairs of alternatives, then the classical objection of economists is that choices between alternatives do not yield behavioral evidence on these differences'. Suppes also knew the economics literature well enough to recognize dissenters like Frisch and Lange. The first task of this section is to strengthen his allusive comments into an explicit position concerning ordinalism.

Since Suppes promotes the method of representation theorems and thoroughly applies it to decision theory, all his work takes claim (1) of ordinalism for granted. Claims (2) and (3), however, are potentially contentious between him and this doctrine. The statements we have proposed for these claims analytically exclude rejecting (3) while endorsing (2), so that there are only two ways to contradict ordinalism, i.e. to reject (2) and (3) or to reject (2) alone. It is not difficult to locate Suppes' position on this logical map: he opposes *both* (2) and (3), thus departing from the economists' received doctrine more dramatically than Lange and followers do. The last section has listed three contexts for which he considered axiomatizing 'utility differences', and reviewing them, we find that he conceived of the primitive relation $wx \succcurlyeq yz$ in terms of *choices* for all three contexts, and in terms of *preference differences* for at least contexts (i) and (iii). Here is some textual evidence for this conclusion. Suppes performed choice experiments on (i), and although he did nothing of the kind for (iii), he made nonetheless clear a choice interpretation for $wx \succcurlyeq yz$ also for this context (notice the word 'choice' in the housewife passage of last section). Obviously he had a choice interpretation for (ii). He made it very clear that he also supported a preference difference interpretation concerning (i): 'In the intended interpretation, $wx \succcurlyeq yz$ if and only the difference in preference between w and x is not greater than the difference in preference between y and z' (Davidson & Suppes, 1956, p. 262), or concerning both (i) and (iii): 'we assume that a prior satisfactory analysis of preference (as opposed to preference difference) has already been given' (Suppes & Winet, 1955, p. 260). What is not so clear is what he thougt of the preference difference interpretation for context (ii).[19] However, the ease with which he moved from the language of choice to that of preference differences – see, e.g. the quote from Luce and Suppes in the last paragraph – suggests that he viewed the former, in many circumstances, as providing good information on the latter. This is sufficient evidence to locate him beyond the stage where Lange and followers had left the rejection of ordinalism. Although by no means hostile to introspection, Suppes clearly thought that it was possible, and it would be more secure, to document preference differences in terms of choices.[20]

The second, more difficult task of this section is to evaluate the position we thus attribute to Suppes. We first review the three contexts again, focusing on the primitive relations that enter the representation theorems proved for them by Suppes and related writers, and we ask two critical questions concerning these relations. Do they receive a genuine choice interpretation from these contexts? And if a relation receives a genuine choice interpretation from a context, does it also receive from it a genuine interpretation in terms of preference differences?

(i) *Choice under uncertainty.* For definiteness, we focus our discussion on Davidson and Suppes' (1956) axiom system. As we have seen, these authors' primitive is only an indifference relation, and it is taken to hold only for two-consequence prospects, $wAz \sim yAx$, for any event A. Their choice interpretation for such a restricted primitive raises two questions. First, the more common procedures to reveal an indifference relation from choices approximate it by supposing that *strict* preferences exist, and these are not part of the primitives. We may ignore this problem as if it were purely technical. It seems indeed possible to start more generally from $wAz \succcurlyeq yAx$ and restate Davidson and Suppes' axiom system accordingly; this would just liken it to Ramsey's initial sketch. Now comes the problem that 'ethically neutral' events are elusive to the observer: a subject might have a well-defined ordering of prospects $wAz \succcurlyeq yAx$, without ever exhibiting the desired comparison, i.e. $x'A^* \sim y'A^*x'$ for some A^*, x', y'. If this happens, Ramsey's hope of deriving subjective probabilities from choices among prospects collapses entirely. We may, however, take Davidson, Suppes and Siegel's word that this existence problem can be overcome in practice. In sum, with relevant qualifications, we can agree that Davidson and Suppes' axioms are concerned with genuine choices and these adduce sufficient information for utility differences to be ascertainable from them.

We now attack the remaining question of whether these utility differences represent preference differences. As Davidson and Suppes preserve the essentials of the equiprobability argument used in the VNM framework, we can at the same time take a position on their work and this famous piece of decision theory. The trivial equivalence:

$$\frac{1}{2}u(w) + \frac{1}{2}u(z) \geq \frac{1}{2}u(y) + \frac{1}{2}u(x) \Leftrightarrow u(w) - u(x) \geq u(y) - u(z).$$

cannot by itself guarantee that the utility differences on the right side have any meaning, let alone the desired meaning of representing preference differences. The meaning criterion for a property of a utility representation lies exclusively in the interpretation given to the axioms that are used to derive this representation, but neither the VNM axioms nor the more sophisticated Davidson–Suppes axioms can be interpreted in terms of preference differences. These axioms can receive a sense in terms of risk attitudes – e.g. they make these attitudes independent of the lottery or the state of the world considered – and some meaning can perhaps be found to utility differences by following this semantic line, but it is clearly distinct from the meaning of interest here. This straightforward, but powerful argument was made by Luce and Raiffa (1957, pp. 31–34) when the controversy was raging over VNM utility.[21] It can be refined by adding that, if utility difference could be interpreted in terms of preference differences, on top of their natural interpretation in terms of risk attitudes, this could only result from adding axiomatic material. The supplementary axioms can be spelled out in all technical detail.[22] Of course, the next question will be whether such a reinforcement is purely formal or carries a plausible semantics with it. Whichever the final answer, the fact remains that, in the absence of the supplementary axioms, only the interpretation in terms of risk attitudes can be considered.

Davidson and Suppes do not even consider this objection. They may be excused on the ground that they are primarily trying to extract probabilities, and they identify utility values only with this purpose. Utility values that relate only to risk attitudes, not to preference differences, can fit such a strategy. But it is more difficult to explain Suppes' inclusion of context (i) along with context (iii) into one and the same research programme on utility differences. And elsewhere in his work, he made some definitely unguarded claims regarding the ability of u to measure preference differences. For instance, Davidson et al. (1955, p. 157) bluntly write that axiom systems like the VNM one 'suggest relative simple behavioristic procedures for empirically testing degrees of preference'.

To summarize the case for context (i), this delivers a genuine choice interpretation, but lacking a suitable defence, no interpretation in terms of preference differences.

(ii) *Stochastic choice.* There is no question that this context brings out choice information, since the primitive term $p(w, x)$ comes with the interpretation of the frequency of a particular choice. The controversial part is how to relate the stochastic data to preferences. What we have identified as the major difficulty with (i) is still present here: preference differences do not enter the axiom system, so that the claim that the derived u value permits representing them is unwarranted. The conclusion just reached for (i) holds equally well for (ii).

One may strengthen this dismissal by exploiting an intuitive argument that Luce and Suppes (1965, pp. 334–335) have impartially pointed out. In private correspondence with Luce, Savage had claimed that one could find three options x, y and z with the following properties: the subject wavers between x and y, though slightly in favour of x, wavers between x and z, though slightly in favour of z, but does not hesitate to take z when the other option is y. If probabilities could be equated with utility differences, a contradiction would result. Translating the choice probabilities into utility differences, one would get that $u(x) - u(y)$ is a very small positive number, $u(x) - u(z)$ is another very small positive number and $u(z) - u(y)$ is a quite large positive number. This is a contradiction since

$$u(z) - u(y) = u(z) - u(x) + u(x) - u(y).$$

In other words, utility differences must add up, whereas choice probabilities are not expected always to do so. After a complex discussion, Luce and Suppes acknowledge that they cannot accommodate the objection entirely (see p. 337).[23]

One can question the link between stochastic choice and preference differences by a more direct semantic argument. In general – barring the exceptional 0–1 case – stochastic choice data do not entail the existence of an ordinal utility function. That a strongly unique u exists independently of any ordinal representation is paradoxical from the perspective of utility theory. In fact, stochastic choice theory has been developed for subjects who either do not have preference orderings, or do have ones, but make implementations errors and thus deviate from their preferences at the choice level. It would be very strange to attribute an ordering of preference differences to subjects with these characteristics.[24]

To summarize the case for context (ii), the choice interpretation is unproblematic, but the interpretation in terms of preference differences fails, and this time, we suggest, for deep semantic reasons, and not simply for lack of a proper justification.

(iii) *Choice under certainty*. We begin by a technical move, i.e. the dismissal of the absolute difference representation (**) that Suppes and Winet (1955) axiomatically derive. They need the formidable axiom (labelled A5 in their paper):

$$xy \succsim yx \text{ for all } x, y \in X.$$

In preference terms, this would entail that the subject is indifferent between moving up or down the utility scale, which seems absurd. Some empirical measurements fit the axiom and ensuing representation very well, for instance those involving the distance concept, and it remains a mystery why Suppes did not mention them in his paper instead of connecting his axiomatic with a 'revival' programme that is ostensibly concerned with preferences. A possible explanation is that he was primarily interested in this programme, but did not yet have the right theorem for his purpose. As we mentioned, axiom systems for (*) appear only in his later work. The crucial axiom in these systems is:

$$\text{(A) } wx \succsim yz \text{ if and only if } zy \succsim xw \text{ for all } x, y, z, w \in X,$$

which is of course much weaker than Suppes and Winet's A5.

Having thus cleared the ground, we discuss our two questions in terms of comparisons of Paretian 'transitions'. We have left pending the problem that these comparisons raise when it comes to interpreting them in terms of choices. In one variant, the observer collects comparisons only when both 'transitions' are for the better, and in the other, he collects them in all cases. Let us consider the more encompassing variant first. When the subject does not spontaneously depart from the status quo, the observer will have to *tell him* that he should do so, and force him if necessary. This is a forced choice all right, but is it less of a choice for that? A purist who would complain that the choice information is blurred by the intervention would have to take a sceptical stand on experimental work in decision theory as a whole, since the instructions that experimenters need to give to their subjects are similarly verbal and authoritarian. They create artificial situations that are only remotely related to the subjects' own experiences, and the answers given for these situations nonetheless count as being representative of the subjects' *choices*. To deny that would be to dismiss basic experiments, such as Allais' and Kahneman and Tversky's, whose significance is well established in decision theory. We do not see why an experiment on swapping objects, as in the housewife example, would strike subjects as being stranger than standard experiments on lotteries, which involve the possibly unfamiliar concept of a numerical probability. The consistent purist will have to go as far as to claim that *only non-induced choices count*, as is supposedly the case with market observations. We interpret Lange's and Allen's claims regarding introspection as reflecting this drastic stand, which neoclassical economist often endorsed both before and after these writers. Here Suppes' position as an external observer of economics appears to be a clear advantage.

Another line of argument is available anyhow, which makes it less necessary to discuss experimentation. For (*) to obtain, axiom (A) must hold, and since it is needed anyhow, one may use it as well to convert the information on positive differences into information on negative differences. That is, instead of letting the subject decide between 'transitions' for the worse, one will apply (A) to the more natural comparison made for the better that results from reversing the order of the 'transitions'. Notice that (A) is powerful enough also to cover comparisons between a 'transition' for the better and a 'transition' for the worse.[25] A philosophical discussion may then ensue to decide whether (A) makes sense only for a rational agent or as a matter of definition; this discussion would be reminiscent of the classic one concerning the transitivity of preference, which has been defended in both ways.

We have these two principled ways of defending a choice interpretation for the primitive relation $wx \succcurlyeq yz$ when context (iii) prevails, but we must acknowledge the complication of *motivating* the choices in the course of an experiment. Following the received methodology of experimental economics, if Suppes' housewife is to answer truthfully whether she chooses trading the toaster for the waffle iron, or trading the waxer for the blender, she must be materially motivated to do so. The purist of our previous discussion may change tack and argue in this more pragmatic way. However, it is unclear whether the motivation problem is worse here than it is in basic choice experiments such as Allais' or Kahneman and Tversky's, and the purist may have again to extend his critique farther than he means to.

We now move to the question of whether the relation $wx \succcurlyeq yz$ can be interpreted in terms of preference differences. This is a priori unproblematic, because the axiom systems are geared at this interpretation, unlike those proposed for contexts (i) and (ii), but an a posteriori check may be desirable. It would consist in selecting a system from Suppes' late work, or even better from a recent catalogue of such systems like the one Köbberling (2006) offers, and checking that each axiom in turn can receive a plausible semantics in terms of preference differences. We eschew this task here and just claim that it can be carried out.

To summarize the case for context (iii), it appears to pass both interpretative tests, unlike the others.

The rejection of both ordinalist tenets (2) and (3) seems to be warranted at long last, but we must now explain what kind of utility functions will come out of this rejection and the simultaneous acceptance of tenet (1). In Section 2, we have clarified the uniqueness of the VNM utility function u on X by saying that it is only *relatively* cardinal. The same restriction holds not only for the utility functions obtained by other representation theorems for context (i), such as that of Davidson and Suppes, but also for the utility functions obtained by the very different theorems proved for contexts (ii) and (iii). Since the last context has emerged as the only one of relevance, we consider it exclusively from now on.

Like the VNM representation theorem, those proved for (iii) have an existence and a uniqueness conclusion. According to the former, there exists a utility function u on X such that

$$wx \succcurlyeq yz \text{ if and only if } u(w) - u(x) \geq u(y) - u(z),$$

and according to the latter, u is unique to PAT *in this utility difference representation*. This specific relative uniqueness conclusion actually depends on having included relevant solvability assumptions into the axioms – Suppes' way – or making sufficiently strong domain assumptions – the more standard contemporary way – but we may gloss over this technicality, and just concentrate on the fact that the format restriction is inevitable, exactly as it was in the VNM case.[26]

The previous equivalence can be transformed into

$$wx \succcurlyeq yz \text{ if and only if } \varphi(u(w) - u(x)) \geq \varphi(u(y) - u(z)),$$

where φ is any increasing transform of u, and this states exactly what the generic form of the representation of the quaternary relation is. We can illustrate the consequences for the uniqueness of u by taking $\varphi = \exp$, so that

$$wx \succcurlyeq yz \text{ if and only if } \exp(u(w) - u(x)) \geq \exp(u(y) - u(z)).$$

If we define $u' = \exp u$, this equivalence becomes

$$wx \succcurlyeq yz \text{ if and only if } \frac{u'(w)}{u'(x)} \geq \frac{u'(y)}{u'(z)},$$

and we have checked that, by deviating from the utility difference format, one can find a utility function u' on X that is not a PAT of u, but can nonethless serve to represent the primitive relation. In brief, even with a direct axiomatization of preference differences, the resulting utility function on X can only be *relatively* cardinal.

Does this fact diminish our conclusion that a utility function can combine the three attributes of being purely representational, representing preference differences and having a choice basis? We do not think so. There is no analytic connection between the property of representing preference differences and of being cardinal absolutely rather than relatively, so that we can take the fact in question as making the conclusion more precise instead of contradicting it. It is true that from the point of view of measurement theory, an absolutely cardinal utility function would be a more satisfactory result. If it could be obtained by representation theorems in decision theory, some measurements in this field would enjoy the respectable status of temperature measurement. There are occasional vacillations in Suppes' and Luce's statements of the uniqueness of utility functions, and they suggest that they might have been misled by such physical analogies.[27] With the benefit of hindsight, one may doubt that decision theory will ever reach this higher measurement stage, and the hope seems also forlorn in the related field of psychophysics. For instance, Falmagne's (Falmagne, 2002) book on psychophysics directly defines a utility difference representation in terms of the generic form $\varphi(u(w) - u(x))$.

5. Conclusion

On the occasion of an homage to Patrick Suppes, we have revisited some classic controversies of theoretical economics on ordinal and cardinal utility functions. No doubt a full investigation of this contrast should involve one in considering not only Suppes and his group of collaborators, but also Allais (1994) and Harsanyi (1955), who developed different brands of ideas about cardinal utility, and writers in the classical and early neoclassical tradition, who did not think of utility functions as being obtained by representation theorems. Despite these lacunas, we hope to have brought some conceptual clarity to a still poorly understood debate. By identifying three distinctive claims in ordinalism, which is not usually done, we have been able to contrast Suppes' choice-based cardinalism from Lange's introspection-based form of this doctrine, and by carefully attending to the theoretical and empirical differences between the choice contexts in which Suppes' cardinalism could possibly be implemented, we have finally been able to retain one of his suggestions.

Acknowledgements

The authors are grateful to the editors of the *Journal of Economic Methodology* for inviting this paper, and the second author thanks them for allowing him to pay a personal tribute to Patrick Suppes' leadership and inspiration. The paper was completed when this author was visiting Wissenschaftskolleg zu Berlin. The authors have greatly benefited from a continuous dialogue with Ivan Moscati, as well from Mikaël Cozic's insightful comments.

Notes

1. To our knowledge, the present paper and Moscati's (2016b) are the first to discuss Suppes' utility theory in any detail. Previous homages have emphasized his measurement theory and probability theory, and thus touched on our topic only indirectly (Luce, 1979; Rosenkrantz, 1979).
2. Mongin (2003) has questioned this identification of the axiomatic method with representation theorems. We will however take it for granted here.
3. See Moscati's (2013a, 2013b, 2016a) thorough account of how the cardinal versus ordinal distinction stabilized in economics and decision theory.
4. The *Foundations* uses 'ordinal utility' and 'ordinal preference' interchangeably, and the index of the book refers to both expressions in a single entry (labelled after the latter).
5. On a different score, we do not need to extend our notion of 'ordinalism' to the collective form prevailing in social choice theory and social ethics. The word has been used there quite extensively, still assuming (2) without saying, to deny that interpersonal comparisons of utility are possible (see, e.g. Arrow, 1973, p. 253).
6. On the distinction between a formalization and an axiomatization, see Mongin (2003). Chipman (1971, pp. 327–329) confirms Alt's precedence in axiomatizing cardinal utility (without the word 'cardinal') for the first time. Moscati (2013a) examines how ideas of comparing 'transitions' spread out among economists.
7. A positive affine transformation is of the form $f(x) = ax + b$, with $a > 0$.
8. Whether or not this position conflicts with behaviourism becomes a terminological issue. In his self-retrospective, Suppes claims to adhere to a form of 'methodological behaviorism (…) wholly compatible with mentalistic concepts' (Suppes, 1979, p. 34).
9. This quote is from Davidson and Suppes (1956, p. 159). A similar passage can be found in Suppes and Winet (1955, p. 259).
10. See also Bradley's (2004) reconstruction of Ramsey in fully contemporary style.
11. By a curious contrast, Suppes (1956) defines the quaternary relation $\succcurlyeq$ on a set even larger than Ramsey's, i.e. the set of *probability mixtures* of prospects. As Suppes is well aware of, this contravenes to his principle of taking small domains for $\succcurlyeq$

12. The utility of gambling (which Suppes understands somewhat differently from VNM) is the topic of Royden, Suppes and Walsh (1959).

13. One problem was that the experimental model allowed for an 'error' in the subject's responses, and this turned out also to permit violations of the SEU axioms. Suppes and Walsh (1959) tried to circumvent the problem, but their results were not clear-cut either.

14. For surveys that emphasize this duality, see de Palma and Thisse (1987) and Fishburn (1998).

15. Rosenkrantz (1979, p. 117) interestingly connects this variant with the idea of 'dollar vote' in social choice theory.

16. Fishburn (1970, Chapter 6) restates the problem in this more sophisticated way.

17. This objection appears in Fishburn (1970, Chapter 6).

18. We conclude this from the expression 'due account being taken of the algebraic sign of the difference' (Suppes & Winet, 1955, p. 260). This expression recurs in Luce and Suppes (1965, p. 274).

19. See Luce and Suppes' (1965, p. 334) convoluted comment on two forms of 'strength of preference' in context (ii). This is part of a passage where they present a counterexample by Savage, which we are going to discuss.

20. When commenting on Lange, Alt (1936, in 1971, p. 425) and Zeuthen (1937, p. 237) had passingly contemplated the possibility of collecting choice evidence on preference differences.

21. Allen (1956, pp. 674–675) makes the same point using numerical examples.

22. See Bouyssou and Vansnick's (1990) clear summary.

23. Savage takes x to be a pony, y to be an ordinary bicycle and z to be a sophisticated bicycle. The subject, a boy, cannot make his mind between x and y, or between x and z, but does not hesitate anymore when comparing z and y.

24. We have followed Luce's and Suppes' usual view of choice probabilities. In the alternative conception, randomness takes place prior to the choice level, and is often understood as having to do with what ordering the subject will implement in his choices. It is no more plausible in this conception that utility differences capture preference differences.

25. From (A), if $wx \succcurlyeq yy$, then $yy \succcurlyeq xw$, whence $wx \succcurlyeq xw$ by transitivity.

26. See Basu (1982) for the standard contemporary way of reaching the relative uniqueness restriction. Note that a domain restriction is also embodied in VNM theory, as it postulates a set of lotteries, which are highly structured objects.

27. A somewhat gross example appears in the following passage: 'the various systems developed to represent the expected utility hypothesis end up with the result that utility is measured on an interval scale' (Luce & Suppes, 1965, p. 284). A utility function defined on an interval scale is absolutely cardinal. This is however a rare example; compare with the entirely correct formulation in Davidson and Suppes (1956).

References

Allais, M. (1994). Cardinal utility. In M. Allais & O. Hagen (Eds.), *Cardinalism: A fundamental approach* (Chapter 2, pp. 31–64). New York, NY: Springer.

Allen, R. G. D. (1935). A note on the determinateness of the utility function. *The Review of Economic Studies, 2*, 155–158.

Allen, R. G. D. (1956). *Mathematical economics*. London: MacMillan.

Alt, F. (1936). Über die Messbarkeit des Nutzens. *Zeitschrift für Nationalökonomie, 7*, 161–169. Translated as "On the Measurability of Utility," in Chipman, Hurwicz, Richter, and Sonnenschein (1971), 2, ch. 20, 414–431.

Arrow, K. J. (1973). Some ordinalist-utilitarian notes on Rawls's theory of justice. *The Journal of Philosophy, 70*, 245–263.

Basu, K. (1982). Determinateness of the utility function: Revisiting a controversy of the thirties. *The Review of Economic Studies, 49*, 307–311.

Baumol, W. J. (1958). The cardinal utility which is ordinal. *The Economic Journal, 68*, 665–672.

Block, H. D., & Marschak, J. (1960). Random orderings and stochastic theories of responses. In I. Olkin, S. Ghurye, W. Hoffding, W. Madow, & H. Mann (Eds.), *Contributions to probability and statistics. Essays in honor of harold hotelling* (pp. 97–132). Stanford: Stanford University Press.

Bouyssou, D., & Vansnick, J. C. (1990). "Utilité cardinale" dans le certain et choix dans le risque ["Cardinal utility" and risky choice]. *Revue économique, 41*, 979–1000.

Bradley, R. (2004). Ramsey's representation theorem. *Dialectica, 58*, 483–497.

Bruni, L., & Guala, F. (2001). Vilfredo pareto and the epistemological foundations of choice theory. *History of Political Economy, 33*, 21–49.

Chipman, J. S. (1971). Introduction to Part II. In Chipman, J. S., Hurwicz, L., Richter, M. K., & Sonnenschein, H. F. (Eds.), *Preferences, utility, and demand* (Vol. 2, pp. 321–331). New York, NY: Harcourt Brace Jovanovich Inc.

Davidson, D., & Marschak, J. (1959). Experimental tests of a stochastic decision theory. In C. Churchman, & P. Ratoosh (Eds.), *Measurement: Definitions and theories* (pp. 233–269). New York, NY: Wiley.

Davidson, D., McKinsey, J., & Suppes, P. (1955). Outlines of a formal theory of value, I. *Philosophy of Science, 22*, 140–160.

Davidson, D., & Suppes, P. (1956). A finitistic axiomatization of subjective probability and utility. *Econometrica, 24*, 264–275.

Davidson, D., Suppes, P., & Siegel, S. (1957). *Some experiments and related theory on the measurement of utility and subjective probability.* Stanford: Stanford University Press.

de Palma, A., & Thisse, J.-F. (1987). Les modèles de choix discrets [Discrete choice models]. *Annales d'économie et de statistique, 14*, 151–190.

Falmagne, J. C. (2002). *Elements of psychophysical theory.* Oxford: Oxford University Press.

Fishburn, P. C. (1970). *Utility theory for decision making.* New York, NY: Wiley.

Fishburn, P. C. (1989). Retrospective on the utility theory of von Neumann and Morgenstern. *Journal of Risk and Uncertainty, 2*, 127–157.

Fishburn, P. C. (1998). Stochastic utility. In S. Barberà, P. Hammond, & C. Seidl (Eds.), *Handbook of utility theory* (Vol. 1, Chapter 7, pp. 273–320). Dordrecht: Kluwer Academic Press.

Frisch, R. (1926). Sur un problème d'économie pure. *Norsk Mathema-tish Forenings Skrifter,* 1 (16), 1–40. Translated as "On a Problem in Pure Economics", in Chipman, Hurwicz, Richter, and Sonnenschein, 2, ch. 19, 386–423.

Frisch, R. (1932). *New methods of measuring marginal utility.* Tübingen: Mohr.

Harsanyi, J. C. (1955). Cardinal welfare, individualistic ethics, and interpersonal comparisons of utility. *Journal of Political Economy, 63*, 309–321.

Hicks, J. R. (1939). *Value and capital.* Oxford: Clarendon Press.

Hicks, J. R., & Allen, R. G. D. (1934). A reconsideration of the theory of value. Part I. *Economica, 1*, 52–76.

Köbberling, V. (2006). Strength of preference and cardinal utility. *Economic Theory, 27*, 375–391.

Krantz, D. H., Luce, R. D., Suppes, P., & Tversky, A. (1971). *Foundations of measurement* (Vol. I). New York, NY: Academic Press.

Lange, O. (1934). The determinateness of the utility function. *The Review of Economic Studies, 1*, 218–225.

Luce, R. D. (1979). Suppes' contributions to the theory of measurement. In Bogdan, R. J. (Ed.), *Patrick Suppes* (pp. 93–110). Dordrecht: Reidel.

Luce, R. D., & Raiffa, H. (1957). *Games and decisions: Introduction and critical survey.* New York, NY: Wiley.

Luce, R. D., & Suppes, P. (1965). Preference, utility, and subjective probability. In R. Luce, R. Bush, & E. Galanter (Eds.), *Handbook of mathematical psychology* (Vol. III, pp. 229–441). New York, NY: Wiley.

Mas-Colell, A., Whinston, M. D., & Green, J. R. (1995). *Microeconomic theory.* Oxford: Oxford University Press.

Mongin, P. (2003). L'axiomatisation et les théories économiques [The axiomatic method and economic theories]. *Revue économique, 54*, 99–138.

Mongin, P., & d'Aspremont, C. (1998). Utility theory and ethics. In S. Barberà, P. Hammond, & C. Seidl (Eds.), *Handbook of utility theory* (Vol. 1, Chapter 10, pp. 371–481). Dordrecht: Kluwer Academic Press.

Montesano, A., Zanni, A., Bruni, L., Chipman, J. S., & Mclure, M. (2014). *Manual of political economy.* Oxford: Oxford University Press.

Moscati, I. (2013a). How cardinal utility entered economic analysis: 1909–1944. *The European Journal of the History of Economic Thought, 20*, 906–939.

Moscati, I. (2013b). Were Jevons, Menger, and Walras really cardinalists? On the notion of measurement in utility theory, psychology, mathematics, and other disciplines, 1870–1910. *History of Political Economy, 45*, 373–414.

Moscati, I. (2016a). How economists came to accept expected utility theory: The case of Samuelson and Savage. *Journal of Economic Perspectives, 30*, forthcoming.

Moscati, I. (2016b). Measurement theory and utility analysis in SuppesÕ early work, 1951–1958. *Journal of Economic Methodology, 23*, XY–XZ.

Pareto, V. (1909). *Manuel d'économie politique* [Manual of political economy]. Paris: Giard & Brière.

Ramsey, F. P. (1931). Truth and probability. In R. B. Braithwaite (Eds.), *The foundations of mathematics and other logical essays* (Chapter 7, pp. 156–198). London: Kegan Paul, 1931.

Rosenkrantz, R. D. (1979). Suppes on probability, utility, and decision theory. In Bogdan, R. J. (Ed.), *Patrick Suppes* (pp. 111–129). Dordrecht: Reidel.

Royden, H., Suppes, P., & Walsh, K. (1959). A model for the experimental measurement of the utility of gambling. *Behavioral Science, 4*, 11–18.

Samuelson, P. A. (1938). A note on the pure theory of consumer's behavior. *Economica, 5*, 61–71.

Samuelson, P. A. (1947). *Foundations of economic analysis*. Cambridge, MA: Harvard University Press.

Savage, L. J. (1972/1954). *The foundations of statistics*. New York, NY: Dover.

Slutsky, E. (1915). Sulla teoria del bilancio del consumatore. *Giornale degli economisti e rivista di statistica, 51*(1), 1–26. Translated as "On the Theory of the Budget of the Consumer", in *Readings in Price Theory*, ed. by G. J. Stigler and K. E. Boulding, 27–56. Homewood, IL: Irving, 1952.

Suppes, P. (1956). The role of subjective probability and utility in decision-making. In J. Neyman (Eds.), *Proceedings of the Third Berkeley Symposium on mathematical statistics and probability* (Vol. 5, pp. 61–73). Berkeley: University of California Press.

Suppes, P. (1961). Behavioristic foundations of utility. *Econometrica, 29*, 186–202.

Suppes, P. (1979). Self-Profile. In R. J. Bogdan (Ed.) *Patrick Suppes* (pp. 3–56). Dordrecht: Reidel, 1971.

Suppes, P., & Walsh, K. (1959). A non-linear model for the experimental measurement of utility. *Behavioral Science, 4*, 204–211.

Suppes, P., & Winet, M. (1955). An axiomatization of utility based on the notion of utility differences. *Management Science, 1*, 259–270.

Suppes, P., & Zinnes, J. (1963). Basic measurement theory. In R. D. Luce, R. R. Bush, & E. Galanter (Eds.), *Handbook of mathematical psychology* (Vol. I, pp. 1–76). New York, NY: Wiley.

Varian, H. R. (2005). *Intermediate microeconomics*. New York, NY: Norton.

von Neumann, J., & Morgenstern, O. (1947). *The theory of games and economic behavior*. Princeton: Princeton University Press.

Zeuthen, F. (1937). On the determinateness of the utility function. *The Review of Economic Studies, 4*, 236–239.

Suppes' probabilistic theory of causality and causal inference in economics

Julian Reiss

This paper examines Patrick Suppes' probabilistic theory of causality understood as a theory of causal inference, and draws some lessons for empirical economics and contemporary debates in the foundations of econometrics. It argues that a standard method of empirical economics, multiple regression, is inadequate for most but the simplest applications, that the Bayes' nets approach, which can be understood as a generalisation of Suppes' theory, constitutes a considerable improvement but is still subject to important limitations, and that the currently fashionable 'design-based approach' suffers from the same flaws Suppes anticipated a long time ago. It then sketches an alternative in response, one that differs drastically from the formalisms Suppes endorsed but is consistent with his pragmatic general take on science.

1. Introduction

When Patrick Suppes received the Lakatos Award at the London School of Economics (LSE), Nancy Cartwright, who was giving the laudation, listed all the research interests her colleagues in the Department of Philosophy, Logic and Scientific Method pursued: philosophy of physics and foundations of quantum mechanics, general philosophy of science, mathematical and philosophical logic, philosophy of social science and economics, decision theory, foundations of probability and metaphysics. She then joked that the LSE could save a lot of money by firing the entire department and hiring Suppes instead.[1]

Indeed, Suppes made influential contributions to almost all subfields of theoretical philosophy, including all the ones mentioned above and more. Perhaps less well known among philosophers, but no less significant, are his scientific writings in psychology and economics. The latter include work on utility theory (e.g. a new axiomatisation of cardinal utility theory), rational choice theory (e.g. an alternative to Savage's theory), experimental economics (e.g. the first experimental measurement of utility), welfare economics, the economics of science and the theory of consumer demand.[2]

In this paper, I will address the usefulness of Suppes' probabilistic theory of causality (Suppes, 1970)[3] as a theory of causal *inference* for economics and draw some lessons from it for empirical economics and contemporary debates in the foundations of econometrics. Specifically, I will argue that a standard method of empirical economics, multiple regression, is inadequate for most but the simplest applications, that the Bayes' nets approach, which can be understood as a generalisation of Suppes' theory, constitutes a considerable improvement but is still subject to important limitations, and that the currently fashionable 'design-based approach' suffers from the same flaws Suppes anticipated a long time ago. I will sketch an alternative in response, one that differs drastically from the formalisms Suppes endorsed but is consistent with his pragmatic general take on science.

2. Suppes' probabilistic theory of causality

Patrick Suppes was one of the first postwar philosophers of science to recognise the importance of causality for empirical science, especially social science. While the covering-law model of scientific explanation was already in decline, it took other philosophers another decade or so to put causality back on the agenda and start to work on causal theories of explanation and causal inference (Salmon, 1989). In economics, the development was similar. The use of 'cause' and its cognates was in steady decline from 1930 till the early 1970s in order to rise again, quite steeply, thereafter (Hoover, 2004). It is perhaps ironic that Suppes' theory appeared right at the time when interest in causality in economics was at a historical low.

Against the backdrop of (then) widespread belief in the regularity theory of causality, Suppes starts with the observation that the everyday concept of cause is not deterministic in character (p. 7). The statement 'The thunder caused him to get frightened' does not imply that every time he hears a thunder, he does get frightened. That 'changes in the money stock cause prices to increase' doesn't mean that every time the money stock goes up, prices go up in tandem. Suppes argues that one of the main reasons for the probabilistic nature of the ordinary concept of cause is epistemic: we do not normally know all the factors that affect a given outcome; nevertheless, we describe these partial relations using causal language (p. 8).[4]

Suppes is primarily interested in an analysis of causal relations among *events*, using a notion of event from probability theory. Accordingly, an event is a subset of a fixed probability space. Suppes remains deliberately ambiguous about referring to token events or event-types (p. 79). Importantly, he treats them as instantaneous and includes their time of occurrence in their formal characterisation. Thus, '$P(A_t)$' refers to the probability of event A to occur at time t, '$P(A_t|B_{t'})$' to the probability of event A to occur at time t given that event B occurred at an earlier time t' and so on.

With these preliminaries in hand, we can turn to the definition of a *prima facie* cause. Event $B_{t'}$ is a prima facie cause of event A_t if and only if (p. 12):

(i) $t' < t$;
(ii) $P(B_{t'}) > 0$;
(iii) $P(A_t|B_{t'}) > P(A_t)$.

In other words, an event is a prima facie cause of another event if and only if it occurs earlier and raises the probability of the later event. It is important to note at this point that Suppes maintains that causal relationships are always determined relative to a conceptual framework – which can be given, for instance, by a particular scientific theory or a particular experiment or series of experiments. We will come back to this point later.

The next two definitions concern the notion of a spurious cause. An event $B_{t'}$ is a spurious cause of event A_t in sense one if and only if $B_{t'}$ is a prima facie cause of A_t, and there is a $t'' < t'$ and an event $C_{t''}$ such that (p. 23):

(i) $P(B_{t'}C_{t''}) > 0$;
(ii) $P(A_t|B_{t'}C_{t''}) = P(A_t|C_{t''})$;
(iii) $P(A_t|B_{t'}C_{t''}) \geq P(A_t|B_{t'})$.

Condition (ii) says that the earlier event $C_{t''}$ screens off A_t from $B_{t'}$; that is, once its occurrence is taken into account, the occurrence of $B_{t'}$ provides no additional information about A_t.[5] Condition (iii) eliminates cases where $B_{t'}$ alone predicts A_t with a higher probability than the joint event $B_{t'}C_{t''}$.

The second definition of spurious cause does not demand that there be a single earlier event that screens off A_t from $B_{t'}$ but rather that there be a partition such that every event in that partition screens off the later events. Thus: an event $B_{t'}$ is a spurious cause of event A_t in sense two if and only if $B_{t'}$ is a prima facie cause of A_t, and there is a $t'' < t'$ and a partition $\pi_{t''}$ such that for all elements $C_{t''}$ of $\pi_{t''}$ (p. 25):

(i) $P(B_{t'}C_{t''}) > 0$;
(ii) $P(A_t|B_{t'}C_{t''}) = P(A_t|C_{t''})$.

The significance of the difference between the two definitions becomes plain when one considers a situation where an earlier event affects the strength of a causal relationship between two later events. Suppose that we run an experiment in which individuals are asked to walk along a street to post a letter in the mailbox. On some occasions, there will be a homeless person next to the mailbox, and after mailing the letter they are asked whether they noticed the homeless person ($H_{t'}$) and whether they felt empathy towards the homeless (E_t), see Figure 1.[6]

In the population, $H_{t'}$ is certainly a prima facie cause of E_t ($H_{t'}$ will predict whether an individual feels empathy for most individuals). As psychopaths tend to be better at focusing on the task at hand, it is plausible to assume that clause (i) of the two definitions of spurious cause is fulfilled – that is, degree of psychopathy ($\psi_{t''}$) makes a difference to the likelihood of an individual noticing the homeless. Moreover, holding fixed information about noticing a homeless, it is informative to learn degree of psychopathy in order to determine empathy, so clause (iii) of the first definition is fulfilled. However, clause (ii) is only satisfied for individuals with a very high degree of psychopathy – to whom seeing a homeless doesn't make a difference. Thus, there *exists* an earlier event that screens off the two later events ('very high degree of psychopathy') but it is not the case that every event in the partition ('for every degree of psychopathy') screens them off.

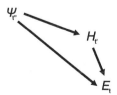

Figure 1.   The causal structure of a psychological experiment.

A prima facie cause that is not spurious is genuine (p. 24). Thus, in the example, $H_{t'}$ is a spurious cause of E_t in sense one, but a genuine cause in sense two.

Suppes goes on to define numerous causal concepts such as direct cause, negative cause and causation between quantitative variables, but they are not relevant to the points that I make below, so I'll ignore them here. Nor will I discuss the counterexamples to the theory, which are widely known and discussed (see for instance Hesslow, 1976; Kleinberg, 2012; Otte, 1986; Reiss, 2015a). The reason is that my project here is not to examine whether Suppes' theory is or isn't adequate as a general theory of causality but rather to assess the usefulness of his approach for causal *inference*, especially causal inference in economics. I will therefore turn to a standard method for identifying causes in economics: traditional regression analysis.[7]

3. Simple multiple regression and causality

A widely used approach to addressing causal questions in the social sciences is to collect data on an outcome variable of interest Y, measure a set of determinants $\mathbf{X} = X_1$, $X_2, \ldots X_n$, and run a regression of Y on $\mathbf{X}$. The functional relation between Y and the X_i's is usually assumed to be linear:

$$Y = \alpha + \beta_1 X_1 + \beta_2 X_2 + \ldots + \beta_n X_n + \varepsilon.$$

A variable X_i is judged to be causally relevant just in case its coefficient β_i is significantly different from zero.

Of course, it is well known that 'correlation is not causation'. Social scientists therefore make sure that enough causal variables are included among the X_i's, or they test the set for robustness and judge as causal those variables that have significant coefficients in all or most specifications.

Neither strategy helps, however, if there are causal relations *among* the regressors or the regressand causes a regressor (cf. Glymour, Spirtes, & Scheines, 1994; Kincaid, 2012). If, for example, the causal structure is as in Figure 2, the coefficient on X_2 in a regression would be positive, even though X_1 doesn't cause Y. If, by contrast, the causal structure is as in Figure 3, the effect of X_1 on Y would be underestimated because only its direct effect is measured, not its indirect effect via X_2.

Two solutions to remedy the situation have recently become popular, one by philosophers and computer scientists and one by a new brand of econometricians. Philosophers and computer scientists have developed a powerful methodology for learning causes from data called Bayesian nets, which can be regarded as a generalisation of Suppes' theory.[8] Econometricians have traditionally sought remedy in theory. Theory is meant to do a variety of things, including determining the functional form of the regression and assumptions about the exogeneity or endogeneity of variables. This programme was largely unsuccessful, however, because economic theory tends to be both unspecific and controversial. There is little agreement on the relevant theory, and

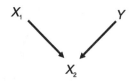

Figure 2.   A causal structure that is potentially problematic for regression analysis.

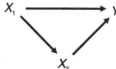

Figure 3.   Another causal structure that is potentially problematic for regression analysis.

most theories are not strong enough to make definite prescriptions about the specifics of the regression equation.

In response to these problems with traditional econometric analysis (also known as structural or Cowles Commission econometrics), a contemporary movement takes experiments as paradigmatic. As certain kinds of experiments are the 'gold standard' for causal inference, they propose to confine econometric analyses to data-sets that have been designed in such a way as to mimic controlled or randomised experiments. The next two sections will review these two proposals and discuss their major drawbacks.

4. Bayesian nets and economics

A Bayes' net consists of a directed acyclic graph (DAG) whose nodes are variables included in the set **V**, and a probability distribution over the variables in the graph. **V** is normally assumed to be 'causally sufficient' – that is, it is assumed that every variable that influences two or more variables in **V** is itself in **V**. The graphs in Figures 2 and 3 are examples of DAGs, with **V** = $\{X_1, X_2, Y\}$. A graph is directed when all edges between nodes are directed (as in Figures 2 and 3), and it is acyclic when there are no loops in which a variable causes itself. For instance, if the arrow between X_1 and Y in Figure 3 pointed the other way, the graph would by cyclic.

The theory of Bayesian nets is closely related to Suppes' theory of probabilistic causality in that it also begins with principles that describe conceptual relations between probability and causality, and these principles are generalisations of some of Suppes' ideas. There are two main principles, the causal Markov condition and Faithfulness. I will now explain what they say and show how they are generalisations of Suppes' theory. To state them, we need the notions of parents and descendants: **Parents**(W) is the set of direct causes of W in **V**; **Descendants**(W) is W together with the set of variables in **V** that can be reached from W by any directed path starting from W. In Figure 2, X_1 and Y are the parents of X_2; in Figure 3, X_1, X_2 and Y are all descendants of X_1.

Causal Markov condition

Let G be a DAG with variable set **V** and P be a probability distribution over the variables in **V** generated by the causal structure G. G and P then satisfy the Causal Markov Condition (CMC) if and only if for every W in **V**, W is independent of (**V\Descendants**(W) ∪ **Parents**(W)) given **Parents**(W).

In other words, every variable in W in **V** is independent of every other variable in **V** except its own descendants (and, trivially, its parents), given its parents. One implication of the CMC is that common causes screen off their effects from each other – an idea also used by Suppes. Another is that mediating links in a causal chain screen off subsequent from prior causes – an idea Suppes uses in his definition of 'direct cause', which hasn't been discussed above.

Faithfulness condition

The second fundamental principle is the Faithfulness Condition (FC), which is the converse of the CMC: A DAG G and a probability distribution P satisfy the FC if and only if *only* those conditional independencies are true in P that are entailed by the CMC applied to G. The CMC says that given a causal graph, certain probabilistic independence relations should hold; the FC says that there are no additional probabilistic independencies.

The FC implies, among other things, that causal relations always result in probability changes. In causal structures such as that of Figure 3, it is possible that a (say) negative direct effect of X_1 on Y is counteracted by a positive indirect effect via X_2. If so, the result may be that X_1 and Y are probabilistically independent despite being causally related. Such a probability distribution would be called 'unfaithful' to the graph. In Suppes' theory, this situation is assumed away by the stipulation that every cause must be a prima facie cause. Some people argue that violations of Faithfulness are extremely rare (Spirtes, Glymour, & Scheines, 2000). But they might not be. When systems have backup causes, a cause might appear to be independent from its effect. For example, when multiple genes produce a phenotype, we can inactivate one gene but the phenotype will still be present (Kleinberg, 2016, p. 108). To give an economics example, a policy that effectively stabilises a target quality (such as inflation), will result in an independence of cause and effect that is in fact the result of a successful exploitation of the causal relation (Hoover, 2001)!

The Bayesian networks approach is more flexible than standard multiple regression. The latter makes the implicit assumption that one of the measured variables (the 'dependent' variable) is an effect and all other variables (the 'independent variables') are either direct causes or play no causal role. The Bayesian network approach allows many kinds of causal relationships among the variables in **V** provided the set is causally sufficient.

However, the Bayesian networks have their own limitations. According to their proponents, multiple regression should not be used in the absence of strong causal background knowledge about the domain of interest; Bayesian networks, on the other hand, do not require this (Spirtes et al., 2000, p. 207; see also Glymour et al., 1994):

> In the absence of very strong prior causal knowledge, multiple regression should not be used to select the variables that influence an outcome or criterion variable in data from uncontrolled studies. So far as we can tell, the popular automatic regression search procedures should not be used at all in contexts where causal inferences are at stake. Such contexts require improved versions of algorithms like those described here to select those variables whose influence on an outcome can be reliably estimated by regression.

Spirtes et al.'s point of view is controversial. For instance, many of the algorithms they use implement the Faithfulness Condition in one way or another: the idea that probabilistically independent variables are not causally connected. As noted, this assumption may not always be met. There is also the problem of using the data to infer that variables are independent since no algorithm, when fed with real data, can determine whether two variables are probabilistically independent. It can measure a correlation and test, against a probability model, whether the correlation is or isn't significantly different from zero. If the test says that the null hypothesis of no difference cannot be rejected, then any of three interpretations can be made: (a) the two variables are indeed probabilistically independent; (b) something 'rare' has happened (how rare is determined by the level of significance); or (c) the probability model is false.[9]

How frequently (a), (b) or (c), respectively, is the correct interpretation of the test result obviously depends on the quality of the probability model we are using. Often the probability model assumes that data are multinomial or normal but economics data are rarely multinomial or normal. Most variables are in fact time series, and correlations are rarely indicative of causal connections in time series (Reiss, 2007). Cross-sectional data often mix populations, and correlations in mixed populations suffer from the same problem (Cartwright, 2001).

It is therefore not surprising that real-world applications of this methodology may lead to nonsense results. Humphreys and Freedman (1996), for instance, discuss a case analysed in Spirtes, Glymour, and Scheines (1993), but not fully reported there, where the graph produced by TETRAD, a programme that implements specific algorithms of the Bayes' nets approach, represents race and religion as causes of region of residence, even though the latter is a dummy variable that is one for 'South' and zero otherwise – which makes neither sociological nor mathematical sense.[10]

One person who would not have been surprised by this is Suppes. While Bayesian networks arguably constitute a development and generalisation of his probabilistic theory of causality, they ignore that the theory made causal judgements always against a framework given by a scientific theory. Purely empirical applications, such as those intended by the developers of Bayesian networks, fall outside its scope. And this is for good reason: unless a scientific theory justifies assumptions such as the CMC and the FC and assumptions about the probability model, there is little reason to believe that they should hold. Suppes comments on the requirement of causal sufficiency made by this approach (Suppes, 1994, p. 363):

> I am myself reluctant ever to commit to having a causally sufficient set of variables. I am too skeptical a sometime Bayesian to think that it is possible to make such an identification. I would certainly agree that when a specific theory is formulated and the random variables and their distributions are given on the basis of fundamental theoretical assumptions, then it is possible, relative to such a theory or, in even more restricted cases, to particular models of such a theory, to identify in a completely explicit and exact way causally sufficient sets of random variables. But this is not the kind of thing to which the analysis of Glymour, Spirtes and Scheines is directed at all. They are really concerned with highly empirical situations for which there is no overriding theory guiding and, in fact, fixing the causal structure. In such highly empirical situations I have skepticism about this notion based upon lots of examples to be found in every area of science.

5. Design-based econometrics

The other alternative to simple multiple regression (and structural econometrics) that has recently gained in popularity as well as influence especially in policy circles is similarly empirical as the Bayesian network approach. It starts from the presumption that randomised experiments are the gold standard or benchmark for causal inference. Thus, in many fields of applied micro economics there is a move towards testing scientific hypotheses experimentally, or, should that not be feasible, to employ quasi-experimental designs. Especially development economics has seen a flurry of work that uses randomised field experiments in order to evaluate the 'impact' of a policy on an outcome variable of interest. The experimental approach has been said to 'have the potential to revolutionize social policy in the twenty-first [century]' just as it 'revolutionized medicine in the twentieth century' (Duflo & Kremer, 2005) and to have brought about a 'credibility revolution in empirical economics' (Angrist & Pischke, 2010).

There are numerous quasi-experimental designs such as instrumental-variable studies, regression-discontinuity analyses and differences-in-differences methods. Of these, instrumental variables are probably the most important and most widely used. An instrument is a variable that: (a) causes the putative cause (or independent) variable; (b) causes the putative effect (or dependent) variable, if at all, only through the putative cause variable (and not through a mechanism that bypasses the latter); and (c) isn't caused by the putative effect variable or any of its other causes. Under suitable sets of assumptions, instrumental variable studies can be proved to yield causally correct conclusions (see for instance Pearl, 2000; Reiss, 2008).[11]

It is easy to see that an instrument constitutes the observational equivalent of randomisation. In a randomised experiment, a randomisation device is responsible for the allocation of subject to treatment groups; the randomisation therefore causes treatment status. As the result of the randomisation (and thus treatment status) is masked from experimental subjects, experimenters, analysts, etc. randomisation shouldn't affect the outcome except through the treatment. Finally, randomisation is genuinely exogenous and cannot be caused by either outcome or any of its other causes.

That randomised experimentation isn't a panacea has been argued a long time ago (e.g. by Heckman, 1992). The list of criticisms is long: randomisation means that there is uncertainty about treatment condition, and since individuals differ in their preferences towards taking on risk, more risk-averse subjects may not enter the experiment to begin with, exit prematurely or get the preferred treatment elsewhere; sample sizes tend to be small so that treatment and control group are likely to be accidentally unbalanced; blinding is practically impossible in social science applications; even if initial blinding is successful, subjects may learn about treatment status if the treatment is effective; randomised experimentation can address only a narrow range of research questions, and to regard it as the 'gold standard' often means that hypotheses are changed so as to allow testing by the method; the method is more costly than alternatives; as a consequence it tends to focus on the short run and ignores important long-run effects.

Quasi-experimental methods such as the analysis of natural experiments and instrumental-variable studies certainly do not create artefacts that are due to the deliberate interventions of experimenters or randomisation. But it has been argued by structural econometricians that they are highly unlikely to yield interpretable and useful results unless the empirical specification is backed up by economic theory (e.g. Deaton, 2010). Let me repeat the main points here. A theory is a fully specified system, and so if a variable appears in the reduced form, we know the mechanism through which it affects the left-hand side variable. There are no other mechanisms than those given by the equations. By contrast, in a purely empirical specification, it is likely that an instrumental variable affects the outcome variable through a variety of different mechanisms, which, in turn, are unlikely to be constant over the different units or structures on which the data are measured. The results obtained are average results over different units/structures, and therefore unlikely to be predictively informative except for new populations that are constituted by the exact same mix of units/structures. In the kind of observational studies that typically use these techniques, this variation can't be thought of as random variation that is uncorrelated with anything else of interest. Moreover, if there is heterogeneity, the result depends on the exact choice of instrument. So what we measure is not the average effect across all units/structures in the population of the study but rather the average among those units/structures that were induced by the specific instrument to assume the value of the putative cause variable that they have. In the absence of detailed information about the population over which the average is drawn here, this is not a very useful and potentially misleading quantity to learn (Heckman & Urzua, 2010). Finally, the instrumental variable estimator will be biased if effect size is correlated with the value of the putative cause variable, which, again, we do not have good reason to suppose is not the case outside of a specific theory.

Now, while I am not aware that Suppes ever commented on this debate between 'design-based' and 'structuralist' econometricians, it is probably safe to assume that he would side with the structuralists. If anything, my guess would be that Suppes would urge economists not just to use economic theory but develop theories that are strong enough to have implications about all aspects of an empirical study that need to be addressed, including independence relations, functional form, error terms and so on, or at least implications that are strong enough so that we have a good reason to believe that tests of the statistical assumptions of lower level empirical models yield informative results.[12]

At any rate, causal judgements are to be made relative to a theoretical framework because outside such a framework there is little reason to believe that the assumptions necessary to validate the judgements hold. Design-based econometrics isn't as neatly laid out as the series of definitions and principles one finds in Suppes theory and in the theory of Bayesian networks, but it equally depends on a variety of assumptions connecting causality and probability, the causal structure of the system studied as well as the functional form of the relationships, the properties of the error terms and so on.

At this point we might think that the arguments of Suppes and the structuralists are at an impasse. The problem is that design-based econometrics itself grew out of a reaction against structuralist econometrics which, in the opponents' view, relies too heavily on economic theory because economic theory is not 'credible'. The problem is not that there isn't any theory, but that there is far too much of it, and economists have a hard time agreeing on which bits are good ones to use in empirical applications. Neoclassical microeconomics can be said to command wide assent in the profession, but this is at least partly due to the fact that it is so flexible as to accommodate an enormous breadth of empirical phenomena. About the case of development economics Dani Rodrik, for instance, writes (Rodrik, 2007, p. 29):

> The main point I take from these illustrations is robust to these fallacies, and has to do with the 'plasticity' of the institutional structure that neoclassical economics is capable of supporting. All of the above institutional anomalies are compatible with, and can be understood in terms of, neoclassical economic reasoning ('good economics'). Neoclassical economic analysis does not determine the form that institutional arrangements should or do take.

Nor do I think that there are too many macroeconomic principles that are both strong enough to constrain empirical implications and widely agreed among economists. In other words, there are good reasons for empirical economists to be sceptical about econometric methodologies that essentially rely on economic theory.

It now seems that we are stuck between a rock and a hard place. 'Purely empirical' methods such as Bayesian networks or design-based econometrics don't work – for all the reasons Suppes anticipated a long time ago. However, the theory-based methodology that he advocated and many still defend today doesn't work in a discipline such as economics either because there is no good theory. Does this mean that causal inference in economics is impossible? There is no space here to develop the idea in acceptable detail, but in the next section I will sketch a procedure for learning causes from data that works, essentially, by reducing the need to make strong background assumptions to a minimum and instead making causal arguments on the basis of a large variety of independent pieces of evidence, none of which would on its own clinch a conclusion.

6. An alternative: statistical minimalism

In this section I want to defend the idea that very simple patterns in the data – simple measures of dependence, ratios, temporal coincidences and sequences etc. – can often give us great inferential leverage when they are based on a deep substantive understanding of the domain at hand. The technically more sophisticated methods of Suppesians, structuralists, Bayesian networkers, design-based econometricians can all be said to produce conditional causal inferences: *if* the scientific theory or statistical and causal or other background assumptions used in the derivation of the empirical specification are correct, *then* we have good reason to believe that the putative cause-variable actually causes the putative effect-variable. In the absence of well-established theories and reasons to trust the background assumptions made, these kinds of inferences are often of limited usefulness.

Moreover, I think that there are good reasons to believe that the problem is here to stay. Economic phenomena are too complex and uncontrollable, research agendas are too varied and shifting, and economic concepts, hypotheses and theories are too deeply infused by values for there being a high chance that a consensus on a broad theoretical framework (one that has any substance) will emerge soon. Situations that are more favourable to statistical analysis can arise in experimental set-ups, but control is often lacking even in typical economic experiments and if it can be achieved, the relevance of the experimental result to economic behaviour outside the laboratory is questionable. Suppes, himself an early practitioner of experimental economics, clearly saw the limitations of the approach (Suppes & Carlsmith, 1962, p. 60 [emphasis original], 77, and 78):

> It is very likely the case that economists will not take the theory too seriously as an *economic* theory. This we are prepared to accept. The evidence for the theory comes from a highly structured, highly simplified experimental situation.

> It may be argued that the data were collected in such a highly structured and oversimplified situation that they have little relevance to economic behavior. This is possibly true, and it would of course be desirable to collect similar data in the field. But then one runs into the problem of lack of control of many variables which are obviously relevant, but which are not as yet incorporated into the theory. It was primarily for this reason that we chose to do the experiment in the laboratory, where it was possible to control many more of these variables.

> Finally, it is certainly true that the theory is at present far too simple to describe much actual economic behavior. The direction of generalization seems clear, although problems, both experimental and mathematical, are present.

There's a tendency for econometric models to get more and more sophisticated from a formal or statistical point of view – no doubt in part thanks to the growing computational power of desktop computers – at the expense of substantive engagement with the subject matter at hand. 'Form beats substance', in a manner of speaking. Many of the younger generation of 'stars' in the profession – Josh Angrist, Steffen-Jörn Pischke, Steven Levitt, to name but a few – seem to be proponents of methodologies to address any economic question (in fact, any socio-economic issue whatsoever) rather than labour or international or public or monetary or ecological economists.[13]

A convincing causal argument cannot be made, however, without very detailed domain-specific background knowledge.[14] Rodrik provides a beautiful thought experiment illustrating this idea (Rodrik, 2007, Chapter 1). He has us imagine an intelligent Martian and ask him to match the growth record of the developing countries against the list of policy proposals that jointly make up the Washington Consensus.[15] Rodrik writes that the Martian would find almost a negative correlation between adherence to the list and economic success: many countries that did exceptionally well (such as the Asian tigers) score low on the list and many of those who closely followed the Washington policies did quite poorly (such as some of the Latin American countries past 1980).

Perhaps this is not so surprising, even from the point of view of someone who has no domain-specific knowledge but knows some of the literature on causality published in the past 50 or so years. Causes are often INUS conditions.[16] That is, causal factors require the right constellation of background conditions in order to be causally efficacious. The Martian's expectation that closer adherence to the list should be followed by higher rates of growth, would be analogous to assuming that the more of the following conditions: presence of a match; presence of oxygen; the match being struck with sufficient force; absence of water; the match being heated up to a certain point; absence of strong wind etc. would be followed by a higher rate of lighting. To reason this way would be silly, even for a Martian.

At best, we should expect that some subsets of the Washington list are perhaps sufficient, but only when they are all present. Maybe there are several different such subsets, such that whenever these factors are co-present, growth will be ignited. Maybe some factors affect not the presence of growth as such but rather its rate (or other characteristics) once it's there. Maybe some factors are causes in some contexts but inhibitors in others. It is at this point that the Martian would indeed need domain-specific knowledge in order to know what he should expect about growth under the hypothesis that the Washington list is a list of causes of growth.

But Rodrik's main point is a different one. He argues that a number of items on the Washington list – protection of property rights, contract enforcement, market-based competition, appropriate incentives, sound money, debt sustainability – should not be understood as concrete causal factors but instead as abstract capacities or abilities of an economy that can be implemented in a variety of different concrete institutions, and in order to work, these institutions have to respond to local constraints and opportunities. If that is so, it is neither immediately obvious whether a causal factor such as 'secure property rights' is even present unless one has the requisite knowledge about what that would mean in the given case, nor would one know what to expect about its growth effects without that knowledge.

The reliability of a causal argument, then, derives from substantive background information and not from the formal properties of inference techniques that are being used (cf. Norton, 2003 on induction). An alternative to the currently fashionable (strongly[17]) conditional inferences is to reduce the need for making formal assumptions to a minimum and proceed on the basis of a substantive understanding of the subject matter at hand. Often it is *very simple patterns* in the data – simple measures of dependence, ratios, temporal coincidences and sequences etc. – that can give us great inferential leverage when they are based on a deep substantive understanding of the domain at hand.

I want to illustrate this idea with a piece of a causal argument given by Ed Leamer in support of the claim that the Fed's manipulation of interest rates can cause recessions

(Leamer, 2009). The first thing to note about Leamer's book is that he spends about two-thirds of the book (the first 13 of 20 chapters) not making any causal argument at all but rather telling us about the US economy. This exercise would be to a large extent pointless if credibility derived from design or metaphysical principles rather than substance. But it doesn't, so it isn't.

The causal argument itself is then based on the understanding that the housing market and the market for consumer durables play an important role in the explanation of the business cycle. Housing and durables are both very good predictors of recessions and important enough in size that they could be implicated in causing recessions (Leamer, 2009, §15.3). He also notes that the Federal Funds rate is a good predictor of housing and durables. Of course, this doesn't mean (yet) that it's also a cause of the latter or of recessions, as the Federal Funds rate might itself respond to one or more factors (e.g. unemployment) that also cause housing and durables, and through them, recessions. Leamer then considers the orthodox solution of statistically controlling for such common causes. But that wouldn't be a good idea (p. 248):

> That's like including the cloud coverage in a model that predicts rain on the basis of the rain forecast. If after controlling for the clouds, we find that the weather forecasts help to predict rain, then that must be a causal effect, right? Wrong. That merely suggests that the forecasts and the rain both depend on some other common variables, like the barometric pressure. It only gets worse as we layer in more and more assumptions about how expectations are formed and what kinds of delays are present in the responses, and what is observable by whom. At this point, the usual solution is to roll out some very heavy and very loud econometric cannon to shoot at the causal target. The noise and the brilliance when these cannon are fired utterly disguise the fact they widely miss their mark. But this econometric performance is only a slideshow. The Priests of the Orthodox Economics Church meditate so deeply in pursuit of Enlightenment about the Causal Structure of the Economy that they do not even hear the noise or notice the cannon flashes. Meanwhile, the Fed's belief in their own importance is not at all affected by the cannon blasts or the meditative chants of the Priests.

There's little point in trying to control for confounders in the absence of a good theory that tells us what all the factors might be that influence an outcome, much less using heavy econometric artillery. What does Leamer propose instead? He first tells us to look at the long-term interest rates instead of the Federal Funds rate because housing and durables will be influenced by them, not, or not directly, by the Federal Funds rate. Changes in 10-year Treasury bonds also predict recessions, but the Fed has little influence over them.

The core of the argument is given by an account of the significance of the relation between long-and short-term interest rates. Banks make long-term loans (such as mortgages and personal credits) and refinance short-term (through, for instance, deposits and inter-bank loans). They make money when short-term rates are relatively low and long-term rates are relatively high. The 'relatively' is important here, though: what matters is that and how much long-term rates are above the short-term rates, not their absolute levels. As long as the spread is large, banks will happily give loans, even to borrowers with a high risk of default – as everybody could observe on a grand scale in the run-up to the 2007-crisis. But when the yield curve flattens or inverts, banks must be much more selective in their lending decisions, if indeed they are prepared to make any new loans at all.

It turns out that every single recession in postwar-US history was preceded by a flat or inverted yield curve. The decision to increase the Federal Funds rate causes a recession when that increase leads to a flattening or inversion of the yield curve, this brings about a credit crunch, the credit crunch, in turn, a decline in housing, and the latter spreads to the remainder of the economy.

Let me emphasise that in a sense, Leamer's causal inference is conditional too: conditional on historical and institutional background information about the US banking system and other aspects of the US economy. What it does not depend on is general theoretical principles about the connections between probability and causality such as the Bayesian-network methodology, strong identification assumptions such as design-based econometrics or economic theory such as the structuralist approach. It is a theory-free, but not a background information-free approach. Though I don't have sharp criteria to make the three-fold distinction theory – strong and controversial causal/statistical assumption – substantive background knowledge, there are important differences. Substantive background information is more readily testable and should therefore more readily command assent. Whether or not the Causal Markov Condition is true makes no difference to any possible observation. If it seems to fail, it is always possible to blame an omitted common cause. Claims about the structure of the US economy don't suffer from this deficiency. There may well be differences in opinion especially when the claim is a quantitative one, but there is no reason to believe that evidence cannot in principle settle such differences in opinion. Moreover, controversies about substantive background information will be fruitful. They will involve appeals to evidence and further substantive background information from which we will learn more about the economy. I don't see the same collateral benefit in the philosophical debates about the adequacy of the Causal Markov Condition and its companions.

7. Conclusions

Would Suppes endorse 'statistical minimalism'? In one reading, the approach is radically un-Suppesian. There are no axioms, no formalism and no theory. It is not surprising that Suppes own empirical and conceptual work in this area was confined to experimental set-ups in which human behaviour was constrained in such a way that certain theoretical and probabilistic assumptions could be expected to be met. Outside of such constraints, in the real world outside of psychological and economic experiments, and in particular in the world described by macro economics, such assumptions are invalid.

In a different reading, though, statistical minimalism captures the spirit of Suppes' pragmatic outlook of many of his works in the philosophy of science such as, for example, *Probabilistic Metaphysics* (see also Suppes, 1988, 2010 among many others). While Suppes did like to axiomatise, applications it had to be based on a detailed knowledge of what is going on in the situation the axioms are supposed to describe. Pragmatism tells us to reject ideas that are not practicable or not useful – in the prevailing circumstances. And in the circumstances of contemporary economics, statistical minimalism is the best we can do.

Disclosure statement

No potential conflict of interest was reported by the author.

Acknowledgements

I wish to thank Pierre-Olivier Bédard, Nancy Cartwright, Samantha Kleinberg and the CHESS Research Group for invaluable comments on a previous version of this paper.

Notes

1. Max Steuer, then a reader in in the LSE Economics Department, quipped in a smaller round later on, 'They could indeed fire everyone in the philosophy department and hire Pat instead, but I don't think that that would save them any money …'.
2. For a review of these and a discussion of Suppes' 'methodology of economics', see García de la Sienra (2011).
3. Subsequent references to this work will cite only the page number when unambiguous.
4. This characterisation is consistent with a view that maintains that the fundamental laws are deterministic in nature. This isn't Suppes' view, however. Suppes maintains both that the fundamental laws of nature are probabilistic, and that causality is probabilistic in character (Suppes, 1984).
5. The screening-off idea is due to Reichenbach, see Reichenbach (1956).
6. I describe the example at type-level. An analogous story could be told at the token level.
7. A referee remarked that 'Regressions are not used to identify causes in economics in the sense of determining whether a variable is or is not a cause. They are used, once the direction of causation is assumed to be known (and subject to a lot of well-known caveats with respect to exogeneity), to measure the strength of causes'. This may be true in sophisticated discussions of econometric methodology to which economists of course also contribute. In applications, I often find that cautions are put aside and judgements made without good arguments about exogeneity. I cannot make this point in any detail here but I don't think that it's dramatically misleading to say that there's a difference between practice and econometric theory in this respect, and what I'm describing in the main text is – a good amount of – practice.
8. I do not mean to make any claims about originality here. It may well be, and is probably the case, that the Bayes' nets programme arose entirely independently from Suppes. But this does not contradict the systematic connection between the two programmes.
9. This is, in my view, true even when non-parametric methods are used. Non-parametric measures of association such as Spearman's rho are still measures of correlation and are only valid under appropriate assumptions about the data generating process.
10. I should mention that Spirtes et al. have written a forceful response (Spirtes, Glymour, & Scheines, 1997), as have Korb and Wallace (1997). Spirtes et al. claim relations among the regressors in the example discussed by Humphreys and Freedman are irrelevant to the point they were trying to make, which doesn't address the charge that the algorithms can produce nonsense results. They also suggest that one cannot trust algorithm results blindly and should, for instance, test results for robustness using different levels of significance. This is good advice, certainly, but does not make my claim that the algorithms work only under strong – causal *and* statistical – and controversial assumptions untrue. See also Humphreys and Freedman's rejoinder (Freedman & Humphreys, 1999).
11. Pearl derives this result from assumptions that include the Causal Markov Condition and the Faithfulness Condition (called 'Stability' by Pearl); Reiss uses similar assumptions but does not rely on the 'screening off' property.
12. I take this to be one of the significant conclusions of the seminal paper 'Models of Data' (Suppes, 1962).
13. Self-professedly so in Levitt's case, of course. Chang (2014) laments that economics has taken this turn.
14. For a detailed argument along these lines, see Reiss (2015b).
15. The original Washington Consensus consisted of the 10 items: Fiscal discipline, Reorientation of public expenditures, Tax reform, Interest rate liberalisation, Unified and competitive exchange rates, Trade liberalisation, Openness to direct foreign investment, Privatisation, Deregulation, Secure property rights. It was later augmented by a number of additional items such as anti-corruption measures, flexible labour markets and social safety nets, but there was less of a consensus on these items. See Rodrik (2007, p. 17).
16. Insufficient but non-redundant parts of sufficient and non-necessary sets of conditions. See Mackie (1974).
17. All inference is conditional on a body of background information; to accept this truism is one thing, to make inferences dependent on the validity of strong and controversial assumptions such as the Causal Markov Condition is quite another. Hence, the qualifyer.

References

Angrist, J., & Pischke, J.-S. (2010). The credibility revolution in empirical economics: How better research design is taking the con out of econometrics. *Journal of Economic Perspectives, 24*, 3–30.

Cartwright, N. (2001). What is wrong with Bayes nets? *Monist, 84*, 242–264.

Chang, H.-J. (2014). *Economics: The user's guide*. London: Penguin.

Deaton, A. (2010). Instruments, randomization, and learning about development. *Journal of Economic Literature, 48*, 424–455.

Duflo, E., & Kremer, M. (2005). Use of randomization in the evaluation of development effectiveness. In G. Pitman, O. Feinstein, & G. Ingram (Eds.), *Evaluating development effectiveness*, Vol. 7 (pp. 205–231). New Brunswick, NJ: Transaction Publishers.

Freedman, D., & Humphreys, P. (1999). Are there algorithms that discover causal structure? *Synthese, 121*, 29–54.

García de la Sienra, A. (2011). Suppes' methodology of economics. *Theoria, 72*, 347–366.

Glymour, C., Spirtes, P., & Scheines, R. (1994). In place of regression. In P. Humphreys (Ed.), *Patrick Suppes: Scientific philosopher, Volume 1. Probability and probabilistic causality* (pp. 339–365). Dordrecht: Springer.

Heckman, J. (1992). Randomization and social policy evaluation. In C. F. Manski & I. Garfinkel (Eds.), *Evaluating welfare and training programs* (pp. 201–230). Boston, MA: Harvard University Press.

Heckman, J., & Urzua, S. (2010). Comparing IV with structural models: What simple IV can and cannot identify. *Journal of Econometrics, 156*, 27–37.

Hesslow, G. (1976). Two notes on the probabilistic approach to causality. *Philosophy of Science, 43*, 290–292.

Hoover, K. (2001). *Causality in macroeconomics*. Cambridge: Cambridge University Press.

Hoover, K. D. (2004). Lost causes. *Journal of the History of Economic Thought, 26*, 149–164.

Humphreys, P., & Freedman, D. (1996). The grand leap. *The British Journal for the Philosophy of Science, 47*, 113–123.

Kincaid, H. (2012). Mechanisms, causal modeling, and the limits of traditional multiple regression. In H. Kincaid (Ed.), *The Oxford handbook of philosophy of social science* (pp. 46–64). Oxford: Oxford University Press.

Kleinberg, S. (2012). *Causality, probability, and time*. Cambridge: Cambridge University Press.

Kleinberg, S. (2016). *Why: A guide to finding and using causes*. Sebastopol, CA: O'Reilly.

Korb, K., & Wallace, C. (1997). In search of the philosopher's stone: Remarks on Humphreys and Freedman's critique of causal discovery. *The British Journal for the Philosophy of Science, 48*, 543–553.

Leamer, E. (2009). *Macroeconomic patterns and stories: A guide for MBAs*. Cambridge, MA: MIT Press.

Mackie, J. (1974). *The cement of the universe: A study of causation*. Oxford: Oxford University Press.

Norton, J. (2003). A material theory of induction. *Philosophy of Science, 70*, 647–670.

Otte, R. (1986). A critique of Suppes' probabilistic theory of causality. *Synthese, 48*, 167–189.

Pearl, J. (2000). *Causation: Models, reasoning and inference*. Cambridge: Cambridge University Press.

Reichenbach, H. (1956). *The direction of time*. Berkeley: Unversity of California Press.

Reiss, J. (2007). Time series, nonsense correlations and the principle of the common cause. In J. Williamson & F. Russo (Eds.), *Causality and Probability in the Sciences* (pp. 179–196). London: College London.

Reiss, J. (2008). *Error in economics: Towards a more evidence-based methodology*. London: Routledge.

Reiss, J. (2015a). *Causation, evidence, and inference*. New York, NY: Routledge.

Reiss, J. (2015b). A pragmatist theory of evidence. *Philosophy of Science, 82*, 341–362.

Rodrik, D. (2007). *One economics, many recipes: Globalization, institutions, and economic growth*. Princeton, NJ: Princeton University Press.

Salmon, W. C. (1989). *Four decades of scientific explanation*. Pittsburgh, PA: University of Pittsburgh Press.

Spirtes, P., Glymour, C., & Scheines, R. (1993). *Causation, prediction, and search* (1st ed.). Cambridge, MA: MIT Press.

Spirtes, P., Glymour, C., & Scheines, R. (1997). Reply to Humphreys and Freedman's review of causation, prediction, and search. *The British Journal for the Philosophy of Science, 48,* 555–568.

Spirtes, P., Glymour, C., & Scheines, R. (2000). *Causation, prediction, and search* (2nd ed.). Cambridge, MA: MIT Press.

Suppes, P. (1962). Models of data. In E. Nagel, P. Suppes, & A. Tarski (Eds.), *Logic, methodology, and philosophy of science: Proceedings of the 1960 international congress* (pp. 252–261). Stanford, CA: Stanford University Press.

Suppes, P. (1970). *A probabilistic theory of causality.* Amsterdam: North-Holland.

Suppes, P. (1984). *Probabilistic metaphysics.* Oxford: Blackwell.

Suppes, P. (1988). Pragmatism in physics. In P. Weingartner, G. Schurz, & G. Dorn (Eds.), *The role of pragmatics in contemporary philosophy* (pp. 236–253). Vienna: Holder-Pichler-Tempsky.

Suppes, P. (1994). Comments by Patrick Suppes. In P. Humphreys (Ed.), *Patrick Suppes: Scientific philosopher, Volume 1. Probability and probabilistic causality* (pp. 362–365). Dordrecht: Springer.

Suppes, P. (2010). The nature of probability. *Philosophical Studies, 147,* 89–102.

Suppes, P., & Carlsmith, J. M. (1962). Experimental analysis of a duopoly situation from the standpoint of mathematical learning theory. *International Economic Review, 3,* 60–78.

Suppes's outlines of an empirical measurement theory

Marcel Boumans

According to Suppes, measurement theory, like any scientific theory, should consist of two parts, a set-theoretical defined structure and the empirical interpretation of that structure. An empirical interpretation means the specification – 'coordinating definitions' – of a 'hierarchy of models' between the theory and the experimental results. But in the case of measurement theory, he defined the relationship between numerical structure and the empirical structure specifically in terms of homomorphism. This is rather a highly restrictive relation between models, and therefore he never succeeded in giving his measurement theory empirical content. This paper discusses what an empirical measurement theory will look like if we would use less restrictive 'coordinating definitions' to specify the relationships between the various models.

Introduction

One of Patrick Suppes's most influential contributions is his theory of measurement, which later evolved into what is now the most dominant theory of measurement: the representational theory of measurement. This latter theory was canonized in the three-volume survey *Foundations of Measurement*, edited by Krantz, Luce, Suppes, and Tversky (1971/1989/1990). These volumes present measurement theory as a highly formalistic axiomatic theory. The first version of this axiomatic theory of measurement is the 'Basic Measurement Theory' by Suppes and Zinnes (1963).

This highly abstract theory of measurement is criticized for its abstractness, that is, its lack of giving an account of actual practical measurement. It does not account for measurement procedures, devices, and methods; and it applies only to error-free data, in the sense that it says nothing about handling the response variability in real data. A recent discussion of the representational theory of measurement aptly characterizes it as 'a library of mathematical theorems [...] useful for investigating problems of concept formation' (Heilmann, 2015, p. 788).

Suppes's contributions to the development of this abstract account of measurement is in sharp contrast with his accounts of experiments in psychology, which have a much more practical focus; they are about procedures, devices, methods, errors, and variability. It is as if Suppes was never able to connect these two kinds of studies. This paper is a proposal of how this potential connection could be conceived, based on expanding Suppes's account of experimental practices into the practices of measurement.

According to Suppes (2002), a scientific theory should consist of two parts, a set-theoretical defined structure and the empirical interpretation of that structure.[1] The reason for having set-theoretical structures play a central role is that 'such structures provided the right settings for investigating problems of representation and invariance in any systematic part of past or present science' (p. xiii). Suppes argues that these 'right settings' cannot be provided by any of the logical languages,

> the artificial-language treatment of problems of evidence are inadequate. [It gives] a much too simplified account of the extraordinarily complex and technically involved practical problems of assessing evidence in the empirical sciences. (Suppes, 2002, p. 2)

In addition to his interest in theory structure, Suppes's also emphasized empirical details: particularly those of the experiments in psychology, some of which he had conducted himself. He hoped to extend his work on set-theoretical structures to include an account of set-theoretical representations of data, 'as a necessary, but still desirable, abstraction of the complicated activity of conducting experiments' (p. xiv), but he never managed to complete the project . In his 2002 book, however, section 8.6 'exemplifies' what he had in mind.

This penultimate section of his 2002 book (the very last section is an epilog) discusses Suppes's most recent experimental work on brain-wave representations of words and sentences. He suggests that most of the activities related to these kinds of experiments are actually attempts to 'clean up' the data:

> As in many areas of science, so with EEG recordings, statistical and experimental methods for removing artifacts and other anomalies in data constitute a large subject with a complicated literature. [...] I am happy to end with this one example of a typical method of 'cleaning up' data.[2] (Suppes, 2002, p. 465)

In addition to favoring a set-theoretical account of structure over the syntactic account of theories, he also favored an approach in which the correspondence rules between theory and data were defined in terms of models instead of empirical interpretations of the syntactical terms. Correspondence should be defined – 'coordinating definitions' – in terms of a 'hierarchy of models' between theory and experimental results. This hierarchy of models consists of various levels of models, with the top level being a model of the theory and the bottom level an empirical model. The reason for using a hierarchy of models instead of direct empirical interpretations of theories is that the correspondence between theory and data is 'much more complicated,' in part because 'the model of the experimental results is of a relatively different logical type from that of any model of the theory' (p. 7).

In case of measurement, the empirical model is:

> an abstraction from most of the empirical details of the actual empirical process of measurement. The function of the empirical model is to organize in a systematical way the *results* of the measurement procedures used. (Suppes, 2002, p. 4)

But as an experimental practitioner he knew that these abstractions do not account sufficiently for the various practices of experimentation, so he hoped to supplement these abstractions of the experimental results with abstractions of the procedures:

> It would be desirable also to develop models of the experimental *procedures*, not just the results. A really detailed move in this direction would necessarily use psychological and related psychological concepts to describe what experimental scientists actually do in their laboratories. This important foundational topic is not developed here and it has little systematic development in the literature of the philosophy of science. (Suppes, 2002, p. 7)[3]

In contrast with the acknowledgment of multiple levels of models between theory and data in experimental practice, in his theory of measurement Suppes distinguishes only two levels: a numerical and an empirical level. Moreover, the correspondence between the numerical structure and the empirical structure is defined solely in terms of a homomorphism. This narrow definition of correspondence is in contrast with the more liberal coordinating definitions determining the hierarchy of models for experiments. These experimental models could be different in nature for each correspondence between two consecutive levels in the hierarchy, and thus include other types of correspondence than homomorphism alone. This narrow definition of correspondence in measurement is probably the main reason that Suppes's theory of measurement never has become a theory that accounts for practice of measurement, and remained primarily a mathematical theory.

This paper will explore the framework Suppes set out for experimental practices: as he developed for the experimental results and also as he hoped that someone would develop for procedures, see last quotation. The aim of this paper is to see how Suppes's framework might be applied to measurement practice, with the goal of ending up with an empirical measurement theory. To do so, I will use my own measurement account that does not require a homomorphic relationship between the numerical and empirical level, because the model structures are modular instead of relational.[4]

Models of data

Before I discuss Suppes's hierarchy of models in more detail, it is useful to clarify what Suppes meant by the terms 'model' and 'theory.' Unfortunately his two textbooks *Introduction to Logic* (1957) and *Axiomatic Set Theory* (1960a) do not provide clear unique definitions of models and theories. The *Axiomatic Set Theory* does not discuss models and theories at all, and the *Introduction to Logic* gives three different definitions of a 'model for a theory': one used in logic, one in mathematical economics, and one in empirical science:

> Logic: 'when a theory is axiomatized by defining a set-theoretical predicate, by a model for the theory we mean simply an entity which satisfies the predicate' (1957, p. 253).

> Mathematical economics: 'the model for a theory is the set of all models for the theory in the logicians' sense. What the logicians call a model is labeled a structure' (p. 253).

> Empirical science: a model is 'an exact mathematical theory', and a theory is a set of 'non-mathematical, relatively inexact statements about the fundamental ideas of a given domain in science' (p. 254).

Suppes's habit of listing the definitions of models used in various disciplines rather than providing a single definition of a model was continued in his 1960 article on the 'Comparison of the Meaning and Uses of Models in Mathematics and the Empirical Science.'[5] In that case the disciplines were mathematical logic, physics, economics, psychology, and mathematical statistics, but he also made his preferences more explicit. He considered Tarski's definition as 'a fundamental concept' in all the above disciplines: 'I would assert that the meaning of the concept of model is the same in mathematics and the empirical sciences' (1960b, p. 289). Tarski defined a model of a theory T as 'a possible realization in which all valid sentences of a theory T are satisfied' (Tarski quoted in Suppes, 1960b, p. 287). A theory is thus a linguistic entity consisting of a set of sentences and models are non-linguistic entities in which the theory is satisfied (1960b, p. 290).[6]

It is striking that in these early papers, models were exclusively defined in relation to a theory, evidenced by calling them 'model of a theory,' or 'model for a theory.' It is, however, in the same period that Suppes started to think about models in relation to data, which he called 'models of data.'

Suppes's account of hierarchy of models was introduced for the first time in his 1960 article on the meaning and uses of models. His reason for introducing this idea of hierarchy of models was the 'radical' difference between the 'logical type' of models used in theory and those used in experiment: 'The maddeningly diverse and complex experience which constitutes an experiment is not the entity which is directly compared with a model of a theory' (p. 297). To make a comparison between theory and experiment possible 'drastic assumptions of all sorts are made in reducing the experimental experience [...] to a simple entity ready for comparison' (p. 297). A plurality of models between these two levels could reduce the need for drastic assumptions.

A more detailed discussion of the hierarchy of models appeared in his 'Models of Data' (1962). He argued that this paper was written to overcome the 'sins of philosophers of science [...] to overly simplify the structure of science' (p. 260) by representing scientific theories as logical calculi and then to 'go on to say that a theory is given empirical meaning by providing interpretations or coordinating definitions for some of the primitive or defined terms of the calculus' (p. 260). Instead of this overly simplistic view of how theories are related to data, Suppes argued that 'a whole hierarchy of models stands between the model of the basic theory and the complete experimental experience' (p. 260). A model at one level is given empirical meaning by a specifically defined connection with the model at a lower level. Because the models at each level are of a different 'logical type,' the connections between them will be also of different types.

According to Suppes a systematic account of these connections should be formal, which for him meant set-theoretical. He did not make clear why he took this position ('a general defense of this conclusion cannot be made here', p. 261), but it seems to contradict his more liberal principle acknowledging the difference between logical types of models, and, as will be shown below, it also prevented him from providing an account that would connect all the various levels down the hierarchy.

The lowest level of the hierarchy, however, could not be modeled. This lowest level is that pertaining to 'noises, lighting, odors, phases of the moon,' see Table 1, 'here is placed every intuitive consideration of experimental design that involves no formal statistics' (p. 258). In contrast to this lowest level, the level just above, the level of experimental design, can be formalized, which makes the relationship between the level of experimental design and the level above it (models of data), explicit. This was considered to be impossible for the lowest level because of 'the seemingly endless number

Table 1. Hierarchy of theories, models, and problems.

Theory of	Typical problems
Linear response models	Estimation of θ, goodness of fit to models of data
Models of experiment	Number of trials, choice of experimental parameters
Models of data	Homogeneity, stationarity, fit of experimental parameters
Experimental design	Left–right randomization, assignment of subjects
Ceteris paribus conditions	Noises, lighting, odors, phases of the moon

Source: Suppes (1962, p. 259).

of unstated *ceteris paribus* conditions' (p. 259). In other words, this lowest layer of dealing with the *ceteris paribus* conditions cannot be covered by any model because of the infinite number of conditions one has to account for. Therefore it cannot be connected to the level of experimental design above it.

The level of *ceteris paribus* conditions aims at reducing sources of errors: to mute loud noises, to fresh the air from bad odors, or to reorganize the schedule for observations. These attempts to reduce sources of errors are what I would like to call cleaning activities, since they reduce errors or even remove the sources of them. According to Suppes, these activities, unlike experimental design, cannot be accounted for by any model or theory, and hence cannot be connected to the higher levels.

Notwithstanding that this hierarchy of models account was too restricted to allow for a systematic account of the basic – often most time-consuming – research activities, such as cleaning the environment before any experiment can be run, it is more liberal than the standard view on the relationship between theories and data. In the first place it allows for other types of correspondence rules; and secondly, ignoring the problems of correspondence, the level of the cleaning activities was explicit in the hierarchy. This was exceptional at the time and still is today.

Theory of measurement

During the period when Suppes was developing his account of models of data, he, together with Scott (Scott & Suppes, 1958), was also working on a theory of measurement. Actually his model account is closely related to his theory of measurement, because both were based on Alfred Tarski's theory of models: 'The main point of the present paper is to show how foundational analyses of measurement may be grounded in the general theory of models' (p. 113). The core idea of such a theory was 'to lay bare the structure of a collection of empirical relations which may be used to measure the characteristic of empirical phenomena corresponding to the concept' (p. 113), and therefore the main goal was 'to construct relations which have an exact and reasonable numerical interpretation and yet also have a technically practical empirical interpretation' (p. 113).

To put it in set-theoretical terms, one has to define two relational systems A = < A, R_1, ..., R_n>, and B = < B, S_1, ..., S_n>, where A is a non-empty set of qualitative empirical data, R_1, ..., R_n are relations on A, B is the set of all real numbers, and S_1, ..., S_n are numerical relations such that B is a homomorphic image of A. B is a homomorphic image of A if there is a function f from A onto B such that, for each $i = 1$, ..., n and for each sequence < a_1, ..., a_{m_i} > of elements of A, $R_i(a_1, ..., a_{m_i})$ if and only if $S_i(f(a_1), ..., f(a_{m_i}))$. In other words, a 'reasonable numerical interpretation' of an empirical relational system is a numerical relational system that is homomorphic to this empirical relational system (see also Suppes & Zinnes, 1963, pp. 5, 6).

Forty years later, Suppes (1998) published this theory of measurement in a more transparent but fairly condensed way as an entry in the *Encyclopedia of Philosophy*. Of interest here is that this later account has an additional section on 'Variability, Thresholds and Errors,' which examines the kind of problems that one encounters in the empirical practice of measurement.

Variability in the quantity measured, as Suppes explains, can have different sources. One source can be variability in the empirical properties of the object being measured. The height of a person for example varies on a diurnal basis. Another source of variability lies in the procedures of measurement being used, and this kind of variability is usually attributed to measurement error. Suppes distinguished various kinds of errors: instrumental errors due to imperfections of the measuring instrument, personal errors due to the response characteristics of the observer, systematic errors due to circumstances 'that are themselves subject to observation and measurement' (p. 248), random errors due to variability in the conditions surrounding the observations, and computational errors.

Although Suppes explicitly mentions these sources of variability, he also admits that 'it is not possible here to examine in detail how the foundational investigations of measurement procedures have been able to deal with such problems of errors' (1998, p. 248). However, he gave no such account elsewhere.

A model of *ceteris paribus* conditions

The requirement for connecting the lowest level of *ceteris paribus* conditions to the level above it is the existence of a model representing this level. At this level 'is placed every intuitive consideration of experimental design that involves no formal statistics. Control of loud noises, bad odors, wrong times of day or season go here' (Suppes, 1962, p. 258). The level of *ceteris paribus* conditions is the level of controlling variability, that is, of reducing sources of errors.

Although this level is not accounted for within Suppes's theory of measurement, nor in the more general representational theory of measurement (Krantz et al., 1971, 1989, 1990), it is accounted for by the current metrological theory of measurement. This metrological measurement theory is mainly a practice-based account.[7]

The target of modeling the measurement process in metrology is the measurement function f: In most cases, a measurand Y is not measured directly, but is determined from N other quantities $X_1, X_2, ..., X_N$ through a functional relationship f: $Y = f(X_1, X_2, ..., X_N)$, where $X_1, X_2, ..., X_N$ are called the input quantities and Y the output quantity (JCGM 100 2008, p. 8). If data indicate that f does not model the measurement to the degree imposed by the required accuracy of the measurement result, additional input quantities must be included in f to reduce this inaccuracy (see JCGM 100 2008, p. 9).

The problem with this modeling strategy, however, is that accuracy of measurement does not provide a straightforward way to validate a measurement model. This is because accuracy is defined with respect to the true value of the measurand: 'closeness of agreement between a measured quantity value and a true quantity value of a measurand' (JCGM 200 2012; p. 21). But a true value would only be obtained by 'a perfect measurement,' which is 'only an idealized concept' (JCGM 100 2008, p. 50); therefore, 'true values are by nature indeterminate' (p. 32). This indeterminateness is because there are potentially an infinite number of conditions that can influence the measurand.[8]

> The first step in making a measurement is to specify the measurand – the quantity to be measured; the measurand cannot be specified by a value but only by a description of a quantity. However, in principle, a measurand cannot be *completely* described without an infinite amount of information. (JCGM 100 2008, p. 49)

Regarding this incomplete knowledge of the measurand, current metrology generally acknowledges that measurement should be expressed in terms of uncertainty:

> it is not possible to state how well the essentially unique true value of the measurand is known, but only how well it is believed to be known. Measurement uncertainty can therefore be described as a measure of how well one believes one knows the essentially unique

true value of the measurand. This uncertainty reflects the incomplete knowledge of the measurand. (JCGM 104 2009, p. 3)

Thus, instead of evaluating measurement results in terms of errors, it is now preferred to assess them in terms of uncertainty.

This uncertainty approach has consequences for the way in which measurement models are built. Models should be built 'to express what is learned about the measurand' (JCGM 104 2009, p. 3). Uncertainty, defined as the 'non-negative parameter characterizing the dispersion of the quantity values being attributed to a measurand, based on the information used' (JCGM 100 2008, p. 25), reflects 'the lack of knowledge of the value of the measurand' (JCGM 100 2008, p. 5), and consists of several components, that is, sources of uncertainty.

In metrology the following sources of uncertainty are identified:

(a) incomplete definition of the measurand;
(b) imperfect realization of the definition of the measurand;
(c) the sample measured may not represent the defined measurand;
(d) inadequate knowledge of the effects of environmental conditions on the measurement or imperfect measurement of environmental conditions;
(e) personal bias in reading analogue instruments;
(f) finite instrument resolution or discrimination threshold;
(g) inexact values of measurement standards and reference materials;
(h) inexact values of constants and other parameters obtained from external sources and used in the data-reduction algorithm;
(i) approximation and assumptions incorporated in the measurement method and procedure;
(j) variations in repeated observations of the measurand under apparently identical conditions. (JCGM 100 2008, p. 6)

These sources are not necessarily independent, and an unrecognized causal factor will contribute to measurement error. It is also acknowledged that 'blunders in recording or analyzing data can introduce a significant unknown error in the result of a measurement' (JCGM 100 2008, p. 8), but such blunders are not supposed to be accounted for by the measurement model.

To evaluate uncertainty of measurement results, in metrology the recommendation is to use two different ways of evaluating uncertainty components, a Type A evaluation and a Type B evaluation:

Type A evaluation is the 'method of evaluation of uncertainty by the statistical analysis of series of observations'. (JCGM 100 2008, p. 3)

Type B evaluation is the 'method of evaluation of uncertainty by means other than the statistical analysis of series of observations'. (JCGM 100 2008, p. 3)

Type A evaluation can be objectively established as soon as a metric is chosen, since it is a quantitative concept. Type B evaluation, however, is not based on a series of observations. It is considered to be a 'scientific judgement' based on professional skill 'that can be learned with practice' (JCGM 100 2008, p. 12) depending on qualitative and subjective knowledge of the measurand and 'experience with or general knowledge of the behavior and properties of relevant materials and instruments' (p. 11).

This distinction between Type A and Type B evaluations implies two different stages of modeling, a Type A stage and a Type B stage. A Type A stage exploits the measurement conditions under which the observations are obtained: 'If all of the quantities on which the result of a measurement depends are varied, its uncertainty can be evaluated by statistical means' (JCGM 100 2008, p. 7). A Type B stage depends on 'skilled judgement' and external sources, such as quantities associated with calibrated measurement standards, certified reference materials, and reference data obtained from handbooks, which may be used as an additional pool of information about whether the model is complete. Combined, both stages lead to the following strategy of modeling:

> Because the mathematical model may be incomplete, all relevant quantities should be varied to the fullest practicable extent so that the evaluation of uncertainty can be based as much as possible on observed data. Whenever feasible, the use of empirical models of the measurement founded on long-term quantitative data, and the use of check standards and control charts that can indicate if a measurement is under statistical control, should be part of the effort to obtain reliable evaluations of uncertainty. The mathematical model should always be revised when the observed data, including the result of independent determination of the same measurand, demonstrate that the model is incomplete. (JCGM 100 2008, p. 7)

To arrive at a model of the 'ceteris paribus conditions,' both types of uncertainty evaluations have to be accounted for. Modeling Type A evaluations is no more problematic than any other kind of statistical modeling. The crucial problem is how to model the judgments based on 'other means.'[9]

The basic idea of modeling type B evaluations can be briefly summarized as follows: When modeling the measurement process, one should include every potential input quantity, X_i, suggested by theory, experience, and general knowledge, regardless of whether there are (enough) observations to assume its potential influence. Subsequently the validity of this encompassing model should be tested. The model may still be incomplete, but the tests will tell whether a significant input quantity is still missing or whether the input quantities not included in the model are negligible. To deal with input quantities that are not measurable or for which there are not enough observations for a Type A evaluation, the proposal is to use a gray-box modeling approach instead of a white-box modeling approach.

The relationship between white-, gray-, and black-box modeling is as follows. A white-box model is a set of causal-descriptive statements of how some aspect of a real system actually operates. Testing this kind of model involves taking each relationship individually and comparing it with observations of the real system. As will be shown below, a Type B evaluation does not require this kind of model. For Type B evaluations the model can be a less demanding gray-box model. A gray-box model is a modular designed model, where each of the modules are black boxes. Testing this kind of model does not require having observations for each individual relationship.

To clarify this distinction between white-box, gray-box, and black-box models and the different kinds of testing they require, Barlas's (1996) distinction between three stages of model validation is useful. These three stages are (1) direct structure tests, (2) structure-oriented behavior tests, and (3) behavior pattern tests. *Direct structure tests* assess the validity of the model structure, by direct comparison with knowledge about the real system structure. This involves taking each relationship individually and comparing it with available knowledge about the real system. *Structure-oriented behavior tests* assess the validity of the structure indirectly, by applying certain behavior tests on model-generated behavior patterns. These tests involve simulation, and can be applied to the entire model, as well as to isolated sub-models of it. 'These are "strong" behavior tests that can help the modeler uncover potential structural flaws' (Barlas, 1996, p. 191). *Behavior pattern tests* do not evaluate the validity of the model structure, either directly or indirectly, but measure how accurately the model can reproduce the major behavior patterns exhibited by the real system.

For white-box models all three stages are equally important, while for black-box models it is only the last stage of behavior pattern tests that matters. Barlas (1996) does not refer to gray-box models. Although Barlas emphasizes that structure-oriented behavior tests are designed to evaluate the validity of the model structure, his usage of the notion of structure with respect to these tests allows for a notion of structure that is not limited to realistic descriptions of real systems; it also includes other kinds of arrangements like modular organizations. Structure-oriented behavior tests are also adequate for the validation of modular-designed models and for these models the term structure refers to the way the modules are assembled.

A module is a self-contained component (to be treated as a black box) with a standard interface to other components within a system. I call these modular-designed models gray-box models and they should pass the structure-oriented behavior tests and the behavior pattern tests.

This concept of a gray-box model and the way it should be validated is useful for outlining how to account for the lowest level of Suppes's hierarchy of models. The first step is to acknowledge that the model of the *ceteris paribus* conditions does not need to be a complete representation of the relational system of these conditions, that is, a white-box model. It is not required that the *ceteris paribus* model has to capture detailed statistical knowledge about the complete set of the input quantities and the relations between them. Notwithstanding these weaker requirements on knowledge of these conditions and available observations, strong validation test – structure-oriented behavior tests – exist that are able to identify and even to estimate the magnitude of the uncertainty of neglected, ignored, or unknown influence quantities. As a consequence, the model of the *ceteris paribus* conditions can be a validated gray-box model, which does not require that an infinite number of conditions be accounted for, and moreover, the involvement of 'intuitive considerations that involve no formal statistics' can nevertheless be validated by structure-oriented behavior tests.

Conclusions: connecting the bottom level of cleaning up activities

According to Suppes, a theory of empirical research practices, whether of measurement or of experiment, should adequately account for the complex and technically involved practical problems of assessing evidence. A major part of the activities involved in such research practices are attempts to clean up the data, that is, treatments of errors and their sources. Such a theory should focus more on procedures than on empirical results.

In connecting evidence with theory, Suppes preferred a set-theoretical interpretation of structure because this would allow for a richer account of the correspondence between theory and data than a logical calculus. This account proposes a hierarchy of models as a layered connection between theory and data. The great benefit of such a hierarchy of models is that it acknowledges that models on different levels can be of different logical types. Another consequence is that the correspondences between consecutive models can also be of different types, determined by the types of models that are connected.

While Suppes had developed this challenging framework for a theory of experimental practices, particularly in his account of hierarchies of models, his theory of measurement lacks these features and suffers from too drastic simplifications. One of these crucial simplifications is that he restricted the kind of correspondence between an empirical and a numerical structure exclusively to homomorphisms.

According to Suppes's theory of measurement, the key requirement of measurement is to find a homomorphism that maps the relations between the relevant features of the measurand into a numerical model. This model is a representation of the empirical relational structure. The implicit consequence of the homomorphism requirement is that for the measurement to be reliable, the model needs to be as complete as possible. Completeness means in this case that the model encompasses all possible influences that may affect the measurand. Because the *ceteris paribus* conditions cannot be covered completely by any white-box model (because of the potentially infinite number of conditions one has to account for), Suppes assumed that this level could not be captured by a model at all, and that only 'intuitive considerations' could play a role. The argument in this paper, however, suggests that with specific validation tests – structure-oriented behavior tests – combined with a specific model design – gray box – a model of *ceteris paribus* conditions is feasible. The consequence of this is that the measurement model does not have to be a homomorphism of the structural relations describing the measurand.

Disclosure statement

No potential conflict of interest was reported by the author.

Notes

1. Although this book is published nearly at the end of Suppes's life, it represents his rather invariant ideas as he had developed over many years: 'I began this book as a young man. Well, at least I think of under 40 as being young, certainly now. I finished it in my tenth year of retirement, at the age of 80' (p. xv).
2. An electroencephalogram (EEG) is a test that records the electrical activity of a brain.
3. These 'psychological and related psychological concepts' were not further explicated, but I assume that these are related to the subjective judgements that have to be made while setting up and running an experiment. As such they will be discussed in later sections.
4. This account can be found in Chapter 2 of Boumans (2015).
5. A habit which he actually also continued in his later work.
6. In his later work, Suppes would not anymore attempt to give such a definition of a 'theory.' For example, in his 2002 book in a section titled 'What Is a Scientific Theory,' he answers this question by stating that 'scientific theories cannot be defined simply or directly in terms of other nonphysical, abstract objects' (p. 2).
7. Metrology is a field within instrument and control engineering involved with measurement and is the shared view on measurement of the international metrological organizations. This shared view can be found in the publications of the Joint Committee for Guides in Metrology. These publications are used here to outline this metrological measurement theory.
8. A quantity is very generally defined as 'property of a phenomenon, body, or substance, where the property has a magnitude that can be expressed as a number and a reference' (JCGM 200 2012, p. 2). This definition of quantity is more general than the traditional definition of quantity where it is a property of an object.
9. A more detailed outline of this kind of modeling have been presented in Boumans (2013, 2015). The next paragraphs of the section are based on excerpts from these two publications.

References

Barlas, Y. (1996). Formal aspects of model validity and validation in system dynamics. *System Dynamics Review, 12*, 183–210.

Boumans, M. (2013). Model-based Type B uncertainty evaluations of measurement towards more objective evaluation strategies. *Measurement, 46*, 3775–3777.

Boumans, M. (2015). *Science outside the laboratory. Measurement in field science and economics.* New York, NY: Oxford University Press.

Heilmann, C. (2015). A new interpretation of the representational theory of measurement. *Philosophy of Science, 82*, 787–797.

Joint Committee for Guides in Metrology 100 2008 (2008). *Evaluation of measurement data: Guide to the expression of uncertainty in measurement.* JCGM

JCGM 104 2009 (2009). *Evaluation of measurement data: An introduction to the 'guide to the expression of uncertainty in measurement' and related documents.* JCGM

JCGM 200 2012 (2012). *International vocabulary of metrology: Basic and general concepts and associated terms* (3rd ed.). JCGM.

Krantz, D. H., Luce, R.D., Suppes, P., & Tversky, A. (1971/1989/1990). *Foundations of measurement* (Vols. 3). New York, NY: Academic Press.

Scott, D., & Suppes, P. (1958). Foundational aspects of theories of measurement. *The Journal of Symbolic Logic, 23*, 113–128.

Suppes, P. (1957). *Introduction to logic.* New York, NY: Van Nostrand Reinhold Company.

Suppes, P. (1960a). *Axiomatic set theory.* Princeton, NJ: D. Van Nostrand Company.

Suppes, P. (1960b). A comparison of the meaning and uses of models in mathematics and the empirical sciences. *Synthese,* Proceedings of the Colloquium: The Concept and the Role of the Model in Mathematics and Natural and Social Sciences, *12*, 287–301.

Suppes, P. (1962). Models of data. In E. Nagel, P. Suppes, & A. Tarski (Eds.), *Logic, methodology, and philosophy of science: Proceedings of the 1960 international congress* (pp. 252–261). Stanford, CA: Stanford University Press.

Suppes, P. (1998). Theory of measurement. In E. Craig (Ed.), *Routledge encyclopedia of philosophy* (pp. 243–249). London: Routledge.

Suppes, P. (2002). *Representation and invariance of scientific structures.* Stanford, CA: CSLI Publications.

Suppes, P., & Zinnes, J. L. (1963). Basic measurement theory. In R. D. Luce, R. R. Bush, & E. Galanter (Eds.), *Handbook of mathematical psychology*, Vol. 1 (pp. 1–76). New York, NY: Wiley.

Freedom and choice in economics

Adolfo García de la Sienra

Even though Patrick Suppes made important contributions to utility theory, his final views on economic choice are quite critical of the expected-utility theories of rational choice. The aim of the present paper is to expose in a unified way his final views on economic choice and freedom. These views are part of his conception of causality and rationality.

1. Motivation

Patrick Suppes' views on economic behavior and choice must be understood and explained within the context of his overall conception of rationality. The presentation of this conception is scattered in many places in Suppes' *opera*, but perhaps the most complete statement is found in chapter eight of his *Probabilistic Metaphysics* (Suppes, 1984; PM from now on). His final view on economic behavior (as he told me) was essentially presented in 'Rationality, Habits and Freedom' (Suppes, 2001), but the view presented in this work presupposes the view of rationality, indeed the whole metaphysical conception presented in PM.

The main questions we are concerned with here are the following: (1) How did Suppes conceive and describe the actual process of choice-making by real human beings, specifically regarding economic actions? (2) Did he finally come to believe that some systematic theory of choice-making was feasible, given the extreme complexity of human behavior? (3) What would that theory look like?

2. Rationality

Suppes' general view regarding the unity of scientific disciplines is that there is no such unity: 'Dominant single concepts or unified theories do not exist for any major scientific discipline, not even for most highly specialized disciplines' (PM, p. 185; cf. chapter 6). Hence, in particular, there is no such thing as a unified theory of rationality, and so his use of the term 'the theory of rationality' should not be taken as implying that he has a tightly knit one.

Rather, Suppes' 'theory' of rationality is a pluralistic collage: we might call it R-theory, since it looks pretty much as Hawking's physical M-theory.[1] Nevertheless, he clusters his analysis around two models of rationality that he considers most important.

The first one he calls the Bayesian model, a conception according to which being rational means being an expected-utility maximizer. The second one is the model of justified procedures (MJPs), a view according to which being rational means providing good reasons for the purpose of achieving an end in view.

In analogy with mechanics, Suppes takes the Bayesian model as a kinematical concept, and the MJPs as a qualitative dynamics of rationality: just as in classical mechanics forces were taken as the (efficient) causes of motion, in the theory of rationality the reasons adduced for the purpose of achieving a given end are the causes of action. Typically, a kinematical concept 'merely' provides a *description* of some phenomenon, whereas the dynamical one provides an *explanation* of the phenomenon in terms of certain relevant causes. An historically important example of a kinematical concept in mechanics is Kepler's description of the motion of the planets around the sun. The dynamical concept was given by Newton, who not only said that the attractive force exerted by the sun on the planet was the cause of its motion, but he actually gave the precise mathematical form of such a force. Out of this form, making use of his calculus of fluxions and his fundamental law connecting mass and acceleration with force, Newton was able to integrate the motion of the planet obtaining a dynamically-generated concept that was a good approximation to the kinematical one. This example suggests a general distinction within any theory T, to wit, between its kinematical part, which is normally elaborated independently of its dynamical part, and the dynamically-generated representation of the phenomenon originally described by the kinematical part. In order to avoid mechanical language, let me call the 'dynamical' part of theory T the T-theoretical part, and the 'kinematical' concept the non-T-theoretical part. Clearly, what counts as theoretical depends of the particular theory that is being considered.

An example in economics of the distinction just introduced is the distinction between the observed behavior of an agent and the attempt to explain that behavior in terms of the concept of preference. The observed behavior is a certain description $\mathfrak{C}$ and the explanatory apparatus is a series of assumptions $\mathfrak{P}$ on the preferences of the agent. Out of $\mathfrak{P}$ a description $\hat{\mathfrak{C}}$ of the behavior is generated and the explanation is considered successful if $\hat{\mathfrak{C}}$ approximates $\mathfrak{C}$ to an acceptable degree. I will assume that the non-T-theoretical part of R-theory is a suitable description of actions actually performed by an agent or agents (I will propose a specific form for this later).

In terms of this distinction, Suppes seems to be saying that the non-T-theoretical (the 'kinematical') part of R-theory is a description of the rationality of the agent in terms of expected-utility maximization. But I think that this analogy is actually wrong, because expected-utility maximization is also a dynamical concept that intends to explain the behavior of the agent appealing to the reasons yielded by expected-utility maximization as the 'cause' of such behavior. Expected-utility maximization seems to be rather a *particular case* of the MJPs, even though Suppes says that 'it is not clear that these two concepts can always be put together in satisfactory form' (PM, p. 208).

Another problem is the equating of reasons with causes. As John Searle – among others – has argued, there is a gap between the reasons an agent has to act and the action itself. According to Searle, the gap can be seen in human action in two ways: forward and backward.

> Forward: the gap is that feature of our conscious decision making and acting where we sense alternative future decisions and actions as causally open to us. Backward: the gap is that feature of conscious decision making and acting whereby the reasons preceding the

decisions and the actions are not experienced by the agent as setting causally sufficient conditions for the decisions and actions. (Searle, 2001, p. 62)

This is not to deny that reasons can become causes; they can, but only if they are made effective by the agent. What Searle wants to stress is that it is the will of the agent what makes reasons become effective as causes for action, as he chooses which ones he will act on. I think that Suppes would not have had any problem with the claim that they become causes when chosen by the agent.

Taking into account the former provisos, we can proceed to present and discuss in some detail Suppes R-theory. One of the central notions of R-theory is the concept of an end, which Suppes took basically from Aristotle's *Nicomachean Ethics*. The Philosopher starts this book stating that

every art and every inquiry, and similarly every action and pursuit, is thought to aim at some good; and for this reason the good has rightly been declared to be that at which all things aim. (1094^a1; I follow the translation in Barnes 1984)

Suppes says that 'there is an ambiguity in the Aristotelian view as to whether good reasons can be given for ultimate ends, but this rather delicate point is not dealt with here' (PM, p. 185). Some philosophers might argue that Aristotle's ethical theory attempts to provide good reasons for ultimate ends, but at any rate Suppes – as far as I can tell – never dealt with the question whether reasons can be given for ultimate ends in life. At least in PM he decided to ignore 'the many tangled issues involving reasoning about ends that are not instrumental for other ends [...] although important, they are not central to the main problems considered in this chapter' (PM, p. 185). Hence, if Suppes R-theory leaves out of consideration reasoning about non-instrumental ends, he is even farther from considering reasoning about moral values. Suppes never developed a theory of moral value and so his R-theory leaves out what Weber (1947, p. 115) called *Wertrationalität*.

This does not mean that Suppes claims that every action and pursuit is thought to aim at some previously prescribed end. As we shall see, R-theory makes room for three types of justified procedures: perfectly justified procedures, imperfectly justified procedures, and purely justified procedures. A *perfectly justified procedure* obtains when there is an independent criteria for judging the result and the procedure guarantees obtaining the result. An *imperfectly justified procedure* occurs whenever there is an independent criterion for judging the result, but the procedure does not guarantee the result. Finally, a *purely justified procedure* obtains when there is no independent criterion for judging the result, but the result inherits, so to say, the correctness of the procedure.[2] Suppes' favorite example of a perfectly justified procedure is found in the constructions of Euclidean geometry, 'for the fit between the desired result and the procedures used is exact' (PM, p. 193). Examples of imperfect procedural rationality are found in practical arts like surveying or cooking. An example of a pure procedure would be cooking, when following a recipe 'can give no principled guarantee of the results obtained by using it. Experience validates the procedure but not the result' (PM, p. 194). Actually, perhaps a better example would be a case in which an experienced cook blends certain ingredients without knowing, *ex ante*, exactly what dish is going to turn out, but knowing that the procedure guarantees that the result, whatever it is, will be delicious.

The MJPs is put under strain both by purely justified procedures, in which the end is not specifically defined, as well as by cases in which it is not possible to justify each step of a complicated procedure. These are the cases that come under the slogan 'The result justifies [the adequacy of] the means.' They make clear that we ordinarily are not able in any serious way to justify each step of a complicated procedure, and yet we still want to claim that we often judge which complex procedures are rational or sensible and which are not. (PM, p. 197)

The model is further challenged by the existence of random urges that generate certain kinds of actions in people in which the ends are not even conscious. According to Suppes, we

> are driven by our pasts and by our hormones in ways we have no hope of consciously understanding. It is part of a realistic theory of rationality to recognize this fact. Conscious intentions can constitute constraints on what we do, but it is mistaken to think that the bubbling cauldron of our unconscious urgings can be cooled by rational introspection. At the deeper levels we do what we do as an expression of urges that are partly random in character and that we can never fully comprehend in any conscious manner. (PM, p. 209)

We shall see later that the random character of such urges will make feasible a certain theory of rational choice for economics.

Hence, to use Weberian terminology, R-theory does not claim that rationality is exclusively 'Zweckrationalität' – instrumental rationality, which gives place to actions defined 'in terms of rational orientation to a system of discrete individual ends' –, but also *affektuell*, 'determined by the specific affects and states of feeling of the actor' (cf. Weber, 1947, p. 115). We shall see that habits also play an important role in Suppes choice theory and so he also makes room for traditional social action, 'through the habituation of long practice.'

3. The kinematics of choice

In the previous section I promised to propose a specific form for the non-T-theoretical part of R-theory. I propose to fulfill that promise in this section. A suitable description of an action actually performed by an agent must specify the identity of the agent, the options that are possible for the agent during the period of time which is being considered, the situations in which the agent can be placed in different times or places, the options feasible under each such situation, the time and place of the action, the situation actually obtaining for the agent at the time of the action, and the option actually chosen by him.

There are basically three versions of expected-utility theory in the air: the oldest, due to Von Neumann and Morgenstern (1947), based upon the concept of a gamble or lottery (call it (VNM); the most well-known, statistical decision theory (SDT), due to Savage (1954, 1972); and conditional decision theory (CDT), Suppes' favorite version, due originally to Luce and Krantz (1971).[3] These theories suggest a scheme to represent the 'kinematical' part of R-theory. Before proceeding to formulate this representation, I will show that the kinematical parts of VNM and SDT are both specializations of that of CDT. Nevertheless, VNM is not reducible to SDT because, as I shall explain below, there is a postulate in SDT that forces $\mathscr{S}$ to be non-denumerable, which makes the theory inapplicable in the case in which the set of states of nature is discrete.

3.1. VNM kinematics is a specialization of SDT kinematics

In order to discuss the relationships among the aforementioned theories, it will be useful to consider a very simple, stylized case of a decision situation. Imagine a person having to go to a walk in a park when there is some probability of a shower.

This person hates to have to carry an umbrella but hates even more to get soaked, and so the possible consequences of her actions are the following:

$c1$: She does not bring the umbrella and there is no rain (stays dry and does not have to carry the umbrella).

$c2$: She does not bring the umbrella and there is rain (gets soaked).

$c3$: She brings the umbrella and there is no rain (carries the umbrella for nothing).

$c4$: She brings the umbrella and there is rain (carries the umbrella but does not get soaked).

Should she bring the umbrella? A straightforward approach to this problem is to assume that the person can tell how much she likes an outcome over any other, so that her preferences over set $\mathscr{C} = \{c_1, c_2, c_3, c_4\}$ can be represented by means of a cardinal utility function like the one depicted in the Table 1.

The utility of outcome c_2 is well below that of the other consequences, reflecting the distance in preference between getting soaked and any other result. Now, if the person has an objective estimate of the probability q of not raining, then she can compute directly the expected utility of each decision (let f_1 be the action of carrying the umbrella and f_2 its opposite):

$$u(f_1, q) = u(c_1) \cdot q + u(c_2) \cdot (1 - q) = q$$

$$u(f_2, q) = u(c_3) \cdot q + u(c_4) \cdot (1 - q) = \frac{4 - q}{5}$$

According to the expected-utility maximization decision rule, if the probability of not raining is 2/3, it is indifferent for the walker to carry the umbrella or not, but if it is smaller than that number she must definitely bring the umbrella with her.

Given a probability distribution over the set $\mathscr{S} = \{r, \bar{r}\}$ of states of nature (r for it rains; $\bar{r}$ for its opposite), each action or decision in $\mathscr{D} = \{f_1, f_2\}$ induces a probability distribution over $\mathscr{C}$. In the above example, f_1 induces distribution $p_1 = (q, 1 - q, 0, 0)$, whereas f_2 induces $p_2 = (0, 0, q, 1 - q)$.

In order to model the previous situation using VNM, the set P of all probability distributions over $\mathscr{C}$ must be introduced, not just p_1 and p_2, together with a preference relation $\succ$ over P that satisfies the axioms specified (for example) in García de la Sienra (2010). The elements of P are called *lotteries* or *gambles*. Distributions p_1 and p_2 are called *simple gambles*.

P contains, for each $c \in \mathscr{C}$, a gamble δ_c in which c occurs with probability 1. Clearly, in the example, δ_{c_1} is strictly preferred to any other gamble, and any other

Table 1. Utility function.

Outcome	Utility
c_1	1
c_2	0
c_3	.6
c_4	.8

gamble is strictly preferred to δ_{c_2}. The axioms of VNM imply that each such lottery is indifferent to some convex combination of the extreme (the most and the least preferred) lotteries. Thus, for each $c \in \mathscr{C}$ there is a number γ such that

$$\delta_c \sim \gamma \delta_{c_1} + (1 - \gamma)\delta_{c_2}.$$

VNM defines the utility $u(c)$ of outcome c as the number γ and establishes the following representation theorem (where supp (p), the support of distribution p, is the set of all elements $c \in \mathscr{C}$ with $p(c) > 0$).

THEOREM. *For any gambles* $p, p' \in P$:

$$p \succ p' \text{ iff } \sum_{c \in \text{supp}(p)} u(c)p(c) > \sum_{c' \in \text{supp}(p')} u(c')p(c').$$

If u' is any other such function, there exist constants $\alpha > 0$ and β such that $u' = \alpha u + \beta$.[4]

$\sum_{c \in \text{supp}(p)} u(c)p(c)$ denotes the expected utility, $u(p)$, of gamble p for the agent. In the particular cases of p_1 and p_2, we have:

$$u(p_1) = \sum_{c \in \text{supp}(p_1)} u(c)p(c)$$
$$= u(c_1) \cdot q + u(c_2) \cdot (1 - q)$$
$$= u(f_1, q)$$

and

$$u(p_2) = \sum_{c \in \text{supp}(p_2)} u(c)p(c)$$
$$= u(c_1) \cdot q + u(c_2) \cdot (1 - q)$$
$$= u(f_2, q)$$

Thus, starting from a qualitative preference relation over the set of gambles, VNM yields a numerical representation in terms of expected utilities that preserves such a relation and recovers the intuition of the example.

The main shortcoming of VNM is that it can be applied only to finite sets of consequences and states of nature. Savage's SDT (Savage, 1972) overcomes this shortcoming introducing as primitive terms a set $\mathscr{S}$ of states of nature relevant to the decision-taker. These states are mutually exclusive and exhaust all possibilities. The second primitive term is a set of decisions or actions $\mathscr{D}$, represented by functions mapping each state in $\mathscr{S}$ with a certain consequence in the set $\mathscr{C}$ of all consequences; that is, if the agent chooses action f and state $S \in \mathscr{S}$ takes place, then a consequence or result $c = f(S)$ ensues. In contradistinction to VNM, Savage supposes that a preference relation $\precsim$ is defined over the set $\mathscr{D}$ of decisions, and derives a qualitative probability relation $\precsim^*$ over the family $\mathscr{F}$ of all subsets of $\mathscr{S}$, defined out of preference relation $\precsim$. Hence the 'dynamical' part of VNM is rather different from that of SDT, but its 'kinematical' part is a particular case of the same, when sets $\mathscr{S}$ and $\mathscr{D}$ are finite. Nevertheless, as I said above, VNM is not a specialization of SDT, because the existence of a probability representation for $\precsim^*$ requires a condition over uniform partitions of equivalent elements in $\mathscr{S}$ (cf. Theorem 1, in Savage, 1972, p. 34) that turns out to be restrictive because it forces $\mathscr{S}$ to be non-denumerable. A n-multiple partition of set $\mathscr{S}$ is *quasi-uniform* if it is a partition of $\mathscr{S}$ in n equivalence classes such that no union of α elements of the partition is more likely than the union of $\alpha + 1$ elements. Theorem 2 (Savage, 1972, pp. 34–35) expresses, roughly, that if there exists a n-multiple partition of $\mathscr{S}$ for arbitrarily large n then there exists precisely one probability measure representing $\precsim^*$. The postulate that there exists such a partition for arbitrarily large n makes the theory inapplicable to the case in which the set of states of nature is discrete.

3.2. SDT kinematics is a specialization of CDT kinematics

The main shortcoming of SDT is that, being the qualitative probability relation determined once and for all by the preference relation over the decisions, the probability of some states of nature may turn out to be positive even if a certain decision precludes them altogether. If (say) an agent having to choose an active from among a continuum of them decides for a specific one, the probability of losing money for those other he did not choose is nil. Yet, SDT still attributes a positive probability to events containing the assets not chosen. CDT avoids all the problems mentioned before and makes room to discrete and continuous sets.

The primitive terms of CDT are $\mathscr{S}$, $\mathscr{E}$, $\mathscr{N}$, $\mathscr{C}$, $\mathscr{D}$, and $\precsim$. As before, $\mathscr{S}$ is the set of states of nature. $\mathscr{E}$ is an algebra of sets over $\mathscr{S}$, but some of the events in $\mathscr{E}$ may have null probability; these are thrown into a set $\mathscr{N} \subset \mathscr{E}$. $\mathscr{C}$ is the set of consequences that are associated to the events. Before each nonnull event $A \in \mathscr{E}\backslash\mathscr{N}$ the agent has available a set of feasible decisions f_A conditional on the occurrence of event A. These can be represented as functions that assign to every $s \in A$ a consequence $f_A(s)$ in $\mathscr{C}$; the functions are not defined for $s \in \mathscr{S}\backslash A$. The 'dynamical' part is a preference relation $\precsim$ over $\mathscr{D}$, and so the other, previous terms should provide the basis for the non-theoretical part of R-theory.

Hence, a specific general form for such a part is a choice structure $\mathfrak{C} = \langle \mathscr{S}, \mathscr{E}, \mathscr{N}, \mathscr{C}, \mathscr{D}, f^* \rangle$. The application of this conceptual apparatus to any agent runs as follows. $\mathscr{S}$ is the set of states of nature that the agent is facing at the particular moment of the choice; it can be seen as a potential sample space. Events having elementary events in $\mathscr{S}$ as members are the members of $\mathscr{E}$; $\mathscr{N}$ is the subset of events in $\mathscr{E}$ having no chance of occurring at all. Each feasible event $A \in \mathscr{E}\backslash\mathscr{N}$ is associated to the family $\mathscr{C}_A$ of all the possible consequences for the agent, contingent upon the decisions available to him given A (and his personal conditions). $\mathscr{C}$ is just $\bigcup_{A \in \mathscr{E}\backslash\mathscr{N}} \mathscr{C}_A$, the union of them all. f^* describes the actual choice of the agent. The restriction $f_A^* = f^* \upharpoonright A$ of f^* to A describes the actual choice of the agent at A.

This concept is analogous to what Richter (1971, p. 135) calls a 'budget space,' which is a structure $\langle X, \mathscr{B} \rangle$, where X is thought of as a collection of bundles and $\mathscr{B}$ is characterized as the family of all 'budgets' that the consumer can face, namely sets of the form $\{x \in X : \mathbf{p}x \leq w\}$, where $\mathbf{p}$ is a vector of prices and w is some nonnegative number representing the income of the consumer. The consumer is represented by f, where f is taken as a correspondence that assigns to each 'budget' $B \in \mathscr{B}$ a set f $(B) \subseteq B$, called the choice set for B, which may be thought of as the set of actually chosen bundles available under budget B. For the sake of the record, the formal definition of a choice structure is as follows.

DEFINITION 1 $\mathfrak{C}$ is a *choice structure* iff there exist $\mathscr{S}$, $\mathscr{E}$, $\mathscr{N}$, $\mathscr{C}$, $\mathscr{D}$, and f^*, such that

(0) $\mathfrak{C} = \langle \mathscr{S}, \mathscr{E}, \mathscr{N}, \mathscr{C}, \mathscr{D}, f^* \rangle$;

(1) $\mathscr{S}$ is a nonempty set;

(2) $\mathscr{E}$ is a family of nonempty sets of $\mathscr{S}$;

(3) $\mathscr{N}$ is a subset of $\mathscr{E}$;

(4) $\mathscr{C}$ is a nonempty set;

(5) $\mathscr{D}$ is set of functions such that, for every $A \in \mathscr{E} \backslash \mathscr{N}$, there is a function f_A in $\mathscr{D}$ with domain A and codomain $\mathscr{C}$;

(6) for every $A \in \mathscr{E} \backslash \mathscr{N}, f^* {\restriction} A$ is an element of $\mathscr{D}$;

It is easy to see that the usual kinematical parts of VNM and SDT can be seen as special cases of this conceptual apparatus. Hence, the kinematics of R-theory can be described as a choice structure.

In particular, the stylized consumer can be depicted by means of a conditional choice structure. Let $\mathscr{S}$ represent the collection of all consumption menus and let $\mathscr{E}$ be the family of all subsets of the form $\{\mathbf{x} \in X : \mathbf{px} \leq w\}$. The family of budgets is $\mathscr{B} = \mathscr{E} \backslash \mathscr{N}$, where the elements of $\mathscr{N}$ are not of the prescribed form. The set $\mathscr{C}$ of consequences is the power set of $\mathscr{S}$. The feasible decisions over a particular budget $B \in \mathscr{B}$ are constant functions from B into the power set of $\mathscr{S}$ (correspondences from B into $\mathscr{S}$) that assign a set of bundles to all the elements of B; i.e. $f_B(s) = C \subseteq B$ for every $s \in B$; $f_B^*(s)$ is the choice set for B and represents the collection of bundles actually chosen by the agent (hence, f^* is just the demand correspondence). According to expected-utility theory, there must be a preference relation $\succsim$ over the elements of $\mathscr{D}$ such that, for every $B \in \mathscr{B}$, $f_B^* \succsim f_B$ for all decisions in the set of feasible decisions f_B conditional on the occurrence of budget B. But the postulation of such a function is a hypothesis that pretends to explain the actual choices made by the consumer and so it would be a *dynamical* theoretization over the choice structure.

3.3. The model of justified procedures

The MJPs is another *dynamical* theoretization over a choice structure describing the behavior of the agent: it purports to explain the behavior of the agent in terms of the pursuing of final purposes, ends or goals. Actually, some philosophers have maintained that, at any time of his existence, a human agent is involuntarily ordained toward ultimate ends, and each of his voluntary acts, which takes always place according to reason and some deliberation, is an effect of the end.[5] In other words, a voluntary act is the result of a decision taken as the conclusion of a deliberative rational process aimed at the achievement of some end. Many actions pursue intermediate ends, ends that are not ultimate but merely means required to reach other ends.

The system of ends of any individual agent can be represented as a finite partially ordered set, and depicted by means of a Hasse diagram as shown in the Figure 1, where the maximal elements are the ultimate ends. The branches are paths of action concocted by the agent to reach the end in the most efficient way and can be mistaken, due to lack of information or proper knowledge of the factors involved. Another factor, that the classical MJP did not take into account, is uncertainty. Hence, the branches must be thought of as action plans that can be modified under the light of fresh information, and subject to random eventualities.

According to MJP, every conscious willful action at a given time t is motivated by the desire to reach an end, given a (dynamically) fixed structure of ends. This leads to

ultimate ends

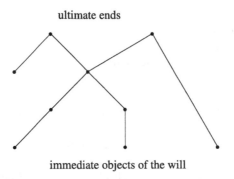

immediate objects of the will

Figure 1. Hasse diagram.

the choice of a path within the structure of ends of the agent. Those actions (if any) that are immediately available to the agent at the given time shall be called *immediate objects of the will*; the other ends are called the *remoter objects of preference*. Thus, the set $\mathcal{D}_t$ of effectively available actions (decisions) for the agent at time t are the immediate objects of the will. Which of these objects will be chosen by the agent?[6]

At any given moment only the immediate objects of the will can be really chosen. An immediate object of the will can be chosen for its own sake, or for the sake of pursuing a remoter object of preference. The elements of the budget set for the stylized consumer are an example of immediate objects of the will, and the preference relation defined over them determines the choice of the most preferred menu. Since these menus are chosen for their own sake (within the confines of the model), they are ends in themselves, and so are not chosen in order to pursue further ends (obviously in real life they might be just means for other ends). But the fact that in the expected-utility models the decisions (or consequences) appear as immediate object of choices, not requiring further deliberation for the choice, just the preference over them, prompted Suppes to see such models as kinematical. That they are not can be seen when we consider choices aimed at remoter ends. The analysis of justified procedures shows that a preference relation must also be defined over the final ends. A final, non-immediately available end can be chosen in a decision situation only if there is an immediate action in the choice set that points or leads toward that end. But then preferring that end involves a deliberation about the procedures leading to it, as well as the belief that the immediately available action actually leads to it. Notice that, even though the notion of preference appears also in MJP and MJP provides a dynamical explanation of behavior, MJP is *not* a Bayesian model.

3.4. The Suppesian model

Suppes' final view on economic choice is presented in 'Rationality, Habits and Freedom,' where he said:

> I have in mind a hierarchical conception of how we make rational choices. To begin with, we must satisfy our habits. With satisfaction of the constraints given by habits we are then left with an unresolved set of choices. How should we choose from this set? The classical utilitarian method is by maximizing utility. The classic algebraic theory I consider a hopeless enterprise .... The rational individual, who is choosing gladly and happily, is one who is freely associating and choosing that one of the available set that seems most attractive,

because of the depth of past associations that are brought up, as can be the case in buying a house, or, in other instances, by the association to anticipated events. (Suppes, 2001, p. 149)

In order to explain Suppes' views on choice and freedom, it will be useful to think of $\mathscr{C}$ as a family of possible objects of choice and each $B \in \mathscr{B} = \mathscr{E} \backslash \mathscr{N}$ as the set of *immediate* objects of the will for the agent at a given time and place. Since habits function as filters that discard possible choices, the concept of habit can be represented as a certain restriction upon the sets within $\mathscr{B}$: its elements would be the sets of choices not discarded by the habits.

Instead of the typical explanation of choice in terms of a preference relation over $B \in \mathscr{B}$, Suppes (2001) thinks that the actual choosing process is more plastic, being based on freedom of association. He quotes Aristotle's and Hume's remarks on association and ends up mentioning the latter's 'three laws of association': *resemblance, closely connected with* and *contiguity.* Yet, there is hardly any systematic view as to how these laws can be used in order to provide an explanation of economic behavior, beyond some general remarks, the complaint that 'there has been far too much separation between the conceptual approaches of choice behavior by economists' (Suppes, 2001, p. 151), and the declaration that he was 'persuaded that the theory of rationality, or of freedom for that matter, in the fullest sense should include the psychological concepts and problems mentioned in the preceding paragraph' (ibid.).

Perhaps the farthest point reached by Suppes in the endeavor of producing a systematic theory of choice that takes associations into account is his theory of random utility. According to it,

> a person chooses the outcome that has the largest momentary utility value at the time of choice, but fluctuations in utility follow some postulated probabilistic mechanism, which, in the present case, would be assumed to be the fluctuations of free associations. (ibid.)

In order to define such mechanism, which for Suppes is a psychological one, assume that the set $\mathscr{C}$ of outcomes is finite with, say, cardinal N. Let $\mathscr{R}$ be the set of all possible regular preference rankings of elements of $\mathscr{C}$. The ranking with more indifference classes contains N (when no two members of $\mathscr{C}$ are indifferent), and so we may take set $X = \{1, \ldots, N\}$ as the image of any utility function representing a ranking in $\mathscr{R}$. In contradistinction to what happens in classical choice theory, where one element $R \in \mathscr{R}$ is singled out as *the* preference ranking of the agent, 'the subjective value of each alternative fluctuates' (Suppes, Krantz, Luce, & Tversky, 1989, p. 421). What this means is that, for each 'budget' B, there is a probability distribution P_B over the family $\mathscr{R}$ of all possible preference rankings over $\mathscr{C}$. For each $c \in \mathscr{C}$ define a random variable $\mathbf{X}_c$ that may take any of the values in X, with joint distribution $\hat{P}_B$ defined by

$$\hat{P}_B(\mathbf{X}_{c_1} = x_1, \ldots, \mathbf{X}_{c_N} = x_N) = P_B(R),$$

where $u(c_i) = x_i$ ($x_i \in X$) and u is the utility function representing R. The system

$$\mathfrak{R} = \langle \mathscr{C}, \mathbf{X}, P_B \rangle$$

is called a *random utility structure* if U is a function defined over $\mathscr{C}$ assigning random variable $\mathbf{X}_c$ to outcome $c \in \mathscr{C}$.

Let $\mathscr{B}$ be a family of nonempty sets of $\mathscr{C}$ and, for each $B \in \mathscr{B}$, let $\mathfrak{R} = \langle \mathscr{C}, \mathbf{X}, \mathbf{P_B} \rangle$ be a random utility structure. Let $\hat{P}$ be the function such that

$$\hat{P}_B(c) = P_B(\mathbf{X}_c = \max\{\mathbf{X}_{c'} | c' \in B\}).$$

Then it is obvious that $\langle X, \mathscr{B}, \hat{P} \rangle$ is a structure of choice probabilities, called the structure of choice probabilities generated by $\mathfrak{R}$ (cf. Suppes et al., 1989, p. 384.). This is obvious because, by construction,

$$\hat{P}_B(c) \geq 0 \quad \text{and} \quad \sum_{c \in B} \hat{P}_B(c) = 1.$$

Quite another problem is whether, given a structure of choice probabilities $\mathfrak{C} = \langle \mathscr{C}, \mathscr{B}, \hat{P} \rangle$, there exists a random utility structure $\mathfrak{R}$ such that $\mathfrak{C}$ is (approximately) the structure of choice probabilities generated by $\mathfrak{R}$. In such a case we would have an analogue of what is usually called a 'rationalization' of a choice structure. An 'observable' condition due to Falmagne (1978), called 'nonnegativity,' is necessary and sufficient for a closed structure of choice probabilities to satisfy a random utility model (cf. Definition 17.14 and Theorem 17.10 in Suppes et al., 1989, p. 423). This condition is an analogue of what in classical demand theory is known as Samuelson's strong axiom of revealed preference.

4. Freedom in economics

In the Third Conflict of the Transcendental Ideas, in the *Critique of Pure Reason*, Kant (1998) explores the opposition between transcendental freedom and the law of causality. Kant conceives this last one as meaning that every state (*Zustand*) 'presupposes a previous state, upon which it follows without exception according to a rule.' This rule is none other than the natural laws (*Gesetzen der Natur*): if state S obtains, then there must be a state S' that produces or generates S according to the laws of nature. Kant conceives this connection in such a way that the existence of S' is enough to keep S in existence, for

> the previous state itself must be something that has happened (come to be in a time when it previously was not), since if it had been at every time, then its consequence could not have just arisen, but would always have been. (CPR, A444/ B472)

The opposite (the negation) of the law of causality is transcendental freedom, which accordingly means the occurrence of an event without a previous cause, that is to say

> an **absolute** causal **spontaneity** beginning **from itself** a series of appearances that runs according to natural laws. (A446/ B474)

An event that is an absolutely spontaneous cause is 'an unconditioned causality that begins to act from itself' (A450/ B478).

Some of the claims made by Suppes in PM really sound pretty much like attributions of absolute spontaneity to some events. Thus, when he affirms that 'the evidence supports the thesis that random or probabilistic phenomena are found in nature and not simply in our lack of knowledge,' criticizing the determinist he adds that, for the former, 'the universe is what it is, and it is not imaginable that events just happen' (PM, p. 29). Hence, Suppes is suggesting that events 'just happen.' The question is 'What does he mean when he says that?' This phrase surely suggests that Suppes is claiming that there are cases of absolute causal spontaneity.

Suppes is not too explicit about this issue. He characterizes randomness in terms of high complexity, takes the position that there is not an absolute dichotomy between determinism and randomness (PM, p. 32), and ends up seeing random phenomena as ruled by laws, although these laws are not deterministic in character:

I defend the following view. The fundamental laws of natural phenomena are essentially probabilistic rather than deterministic in character. (PM, p. 34)

This suggests that Suppes is not denying the law of causality, but rather suggesting a reformation of the same. In contradistinction to Kant who surely conceived the rule governing the causal link as a deterministic law, Suppes would say that that law is usually probabilistic.

A deterministic statement of the law of causality would run as follows.

(1) Every event e of kind K always requires the occurrence of an event e' of kind K' as its cause, upon which it follows without exception according to a rule.

In other words, the occurrence of e' brings about, without exceptions and according to a law, the occurrence of e; and the existence of e requires the previous existence of e'. Another way of saying the same things is

(2) If e'_1 and e'_2 are events of the same kind K', whenever they are placed in conditions $C_1, ..., C_n$ they will produce an event of the same kind K.

A probabilistic reformulation of (1) would be

(3) Every event e of kind K always requires the occurrence of an event e' of kind K' as its cause, upon which it follows with probability p according to a stochastic rule.

On the other hand, a reformulation of (2) would look like

(4) If e'_1 and e'_2 are events of the same kind K', whenever they are placed in conditions $C_1, ..., C_n$ they will produce effects over the same space of possible effects, with the same probability distribution.

But it is not clear that (3) or (4) is what Suppes has in mind when he speaks of randomness in nature. One thing is to say, indeed, that the occurrence of event e of kind K is *caused* by some factor e' of kind K', even though the connection between e and e' is not deterministic, and another thing is to say that e occurs *spontaneously*. More precisely one thing is to say that e' *actually caused* e, even though the occurrence of an event of kind K' causes the occurrence of and event of kind K only with probability p, and another thing is to say that e occurs spontaneously with probability p, *without being caused by any previous event e'* of whatever kind. In his analyses of radioactive decay and causality in quantum mechanics Suppes seems to be leaning toward spontaneity. I cannot imagine him looking for a specific event, within the structure of the atom, as efficient cause of the emission of the particle; or looking for hidden variables in the quantum realm, after the cascade of negative results that he reviews in PM (pp. 23–25). He would say that it is not a matter of ignorance or lack of information, but of the way the world happens to be. Nevertheless, his theory of choice clearly explains behavior by means of preferences, even though the preference relation in force at a given moment is chosen by a psychological random mechanism that has to do with associations and moods.

According to the classical Scholastic conception of human action, only human beings are capable of freedom. Let us take Francis Suárez as representative of this view. According to him, A is a *free agent* iff there exists a system of conditions $C_1, ..., C_n$ such that A does not generate always the same effect when placed in such conditions. Suárez believed that if some cause operates without necessity (i.e. according to a non-deterministic rule), it must have some faculty having the power to prevent its operation, even if all the requirements to operate are fulfilled.[8]

Which one is this faculty of power? Suárez thought that only the use of reason was the adequate root of freedom.[9] But we have seen how Suppes has tried to show, precisely, that even non-rational agents can operate freely in Suárez's sense.

The question is whether Suppes believed that human free acts take place according to a stochastic rule. Again, one thing is to say that human actions have a cause (a motive), that produces the action with a certain probability, and quite another to say that some human actions are entirely spontaneous or emergent. My view is that Suppes seems to have believed that, even though human behavior is not entirely predictable, there are nonetheless patterns that can be depicted as probability distributions. The preference relation in force over the immediate objects of choice (always reflecting a preference relation over the final ends) at the moment is what determines the behavior of the agent.

For Suppes, the first ingredient of human freedom is absence from constraints by other agents, what is called negative freedom: 'The conception of freedom as absence from constraint by other agents has something important and correct about it' (Suppes, 2001, p. 154). But perhaps the central ingredient for him is autonomy, understood as the control by the individual, considered by himself as an end in itself, of his own actions:

> Personal actions fully controlled by another, or by institutions, are not free actions. Intuitively, then, an election or market where there is no choice of candidates or products is not free. (Suppes, 1996, p. 184)

This leads to the concept of relative freedom by means of a ranking of opportunity sets, as it is done, e.g. by Bavetta and del Seta (2001), Bossert, Pattanaik, and Xu (1994), Gravel (1994), or Klemisch-Ahlert (1993). Suppes' measurement of freedom is nothing but a measurement of the choices available to the agent (I guess that it can be proved as a theorem that if opportunity set O is ranked higher than O' then O must have a larger measure than O'). But the dearest notion of freedom and autonomy for Humanism, namely the possibility of rationally choosing the final ends, is eluded by Suppes, due to his reluctance to deal with that topic, as pointed out above. Suppes left the process of choice of final ends shrouded in mystery, perhaps because he felt that he had nothing interesting to say about it, but I suspect that he believed that such ends were not subject to rational choice.

Another important ingredient of freedom for Suppes is uncertainty. An agent may not be subject to external constraints but have an excessive regularity to his habits and act always with the greatest possible regularity in a given area of experience.

> We are very likely to say of that person that he is simply caught up in his compulsions, or his habits if we want to be more generous. But that in any case he is, as far as this area of his experience goes, not free to make a real choice. (Suppes, 2001, p. 155)

An example of uncertainty is the situation of an individual

actually choosing which movie to look at in a modern cable–television environment, where there may be as many as thirty movies at a given moment ready to begin. Here, I do indeed have freedom and, furthermore, it is natural to describe myself as being free, because I have not yet made a choice, and for someone watching me also to say, 'It is uncertain what he is going to choose. He is still free to decide.'

This freedom to choose in the face of uncertainty, at the moment when the agent wants to choose, is opposed to the (implausible) image of an individual with vital ends defined once and for all, and all his decisions taken in advance in view of such ends, so that his behavior is completely predictable. In the language of random-preference theory, this means that it is uncertain which preference ordering will come up at the moment. He may prefer a thriller, or perhaps a romantic movie. Be that as it may, it is always the most preferred item at the moment the one that is chosen among the immediate objects of the will, even if that takes place according to a preference ordering randomly occurring as a result of a stochastic process that depends on changes in the environment and the mental state of the agent. Hence, we may say that Suppes would have agreed with Jonathan Edwards that what determines the will at a given moment 'is that motive, which, as it stands in view of the mind, is the strongest;' i.e. the most preferred one.

4.1.   The measurement of freedom

Actually, at least as far as the agent is modeled by means of a random utility structure, it is clear that the agent's actions are not spontaneous, since he is 'determined' to choose that outcome that has the largest momentary utility value at the time of choice or, as Edwards (1834/1974, p. 520) used to say, it is 'that motive, which, as it stands in view of the mind, is the strongest.' Freedom, for Suppes, lies in the fact that there are several options and that it is uncertain which preference relation will prevail in any future choice situation $B \in \mathscr{B}$, due to the plasticity of associations.

A measure of freedom used by Suppes is the measure of uncertainty introduced by Shannon (1948). The mathematical details are best presented by Khinchin (1957), and so I will follow him here. A *finite scheme* is a probability distribution over a finite sample space $X = \{x_1, \ldots, x_n\}$. If p_k is the probability of event x_k ($k = 1, \ldots, n$) under the scheme, the *entropy* of the scheme is defined as the quantity

$$H(p_1, \ldots, p_n) = -\sum_{k=1}^{n} p_k \log p_k,$$

where the logarithms are of a fixed base (Suppes prefers base 2) and $p_k \log p_k = 0$, if $p_k = 0$. Clearly, H reaches its maximum (over the n-simplex) whenever $p_k = 1/n$, because the function $\varphi(x) = x \log x$ is convex and continuous.[10]

Thus, the agent is maximally free at $B \in \mathscr{B}$, whenever the preference orderings over $\mathscr{C}$ have the same probability. This is the situation in which uncertainty reaches its highest peak. But Suppes also wants to have a measure of the freedom of markets or political elections. Basically, the idea is that the amount of options, as well as the degree of uncertainty in the choices of the agent, are a measure of freedom. For instance, if there are n goods and p_{ij} is the probability that any agent will change his choice from good of type i to good of type j, then a measure of the freedom of the market of these goods is $-\sum p_{ij} \log p_{ij}$. The larger this number, the freer is the market. A study of transition

Table 2. Transition matrix for soft-drink choices.

$n/(n+1)$	Coke	7-Up	Tab	Like	Pepsi	Sprite	D-Pep	Fresca	p_∞	Entropy
Coke	.61	.11	.01	.03	.13	.06	.01	.04	.29	1.45
7-Up	.19	.45	.00	.06	.14	.10	.01	.05	.18	1.82
Tab	.08	.12	.16	.36	.08	.04	.08	.08	.03	2.38
Like	.09	.15	.09	.15	.24	.04	.13	.11	.06	2.55
Pepsi	.18	.13	.01	.03	.51	.07	.03	.04	.23	1.68
Sprite	.11	.18	.03	.07	.16	.33	.03	.09	.10	2.27
D-Pep	.09	.05	.18	.09	.12	.09	.26	.12	.04	2.52
Fresca	.22	.09	.05	.11	.15	.11	.07	.20	.07	2.37
Total entropy										1.85

data observed six times for 264 buyers choosing one of eight soft-drink brands (Bass, 1974, quoted in Suppes' 'Rationality, Habits and Freedom') shows that the markets of Coke and Pepsi are the most stable. The total entropy rate of the soft-drink market – the p_i weighted average of the row entropies – is 1.85 (see the Table 2).

In general terms, given a stochastic process, an indexed family $\mathfrak{x} = \{\mathbf{X}_n\}$ of random variables over a set X with $n = 1, 2, 3, \ldots$, the entropy rate $H(\mathfrak{x})$ of $\mathfrak{x}$ is defined as

$$H(\mathfrak{x}) = \lim_{n \to \infty} \frac{1}{n} H(\mathbf{X}_1, \ldots, \mathbf{X}_n)$$

where $H(\mathbf{X}_1, \ldots, \mathbf{X}_n) = -\sum_{i=1}^{n} p_i \log p_i$ is the entropy of the first n random variables. The data on soft-drink choices are also experimental, but Suppes (also in 'Rationality, Habits and Freedom') includes a study on car choices taken from the US car industry statistics. It is interesting that the total entropy of the national sample is 1.84, a figure quite close to the one obtained under the more controlled conditions of the soft-drink experiment!

Hence, we may conclude that Suppes finally came to believe that some systematic theory of choice-making was feasible, in spite of the extreme complexity of human behavior. As we have seen his theory looks pretty much – not surprisingly – like a stochastic one.

Disclosure statement

No potential conflict of interest was reported by the author.

Funding

This work was supported by Consejo Nacional de Ciencia y Tecnología [grant number 127380].

Notes

1. 'M-theory is not a theory in the usual sense. It is a whole family of different theories, each of which is a good description of observations only in some range of physical situations. It is a bit like a map' (Hawking & Mlodinow, 2001, p. 12).
2. Suppes found the inspiration for this tripartite division of procedures in Rawls (1971, pp. 85–86) division of types of justice into perfect procedural justice, imperfect procedural justice, and pure procedural justice (cf. PM, p. 193).

3. I follow the presentation in Krantz, Luce, Suppes, and Tversky (1971, p. 372ff).
4. The proof is omitted; for a detailed proof of this theorem see García de la Sienra (2010).
5. Cf. Suárez (1961), *Disputatio* 23, S6, §18, T3, p. 769.
6. I am borrowing this concept, as well as others connected with it, from a treatise written by the American theologian and preacher Jonathan Edwards in 1754, 'A careful and strict inquiry into the modern prevailing notions of that freedom of will which is supposed to be essential to moral agency, virtue and vice, reward and punishment, praise and blame' (FW from now on).
8. 'Si aliqua causa absque necessitate operator, necesse est habere aliquot facultatem seu potentiam quae vim habet continendi suam operationem, etiam positis omnibus requisitis ad operandum' (Disputationes metaphysicae, D19, S2, §4, T3, pp. 327–328).
9. 'Adaequata radix libertatis ist usus rationis' (D19, S1, §13, T3, p. 324).
10. For the argument, see Khinchin (1957, p. 4).

References

Barnes, J. (1984). *The complete works of Aristotle*. Princeton: Princeton University Press.

Bass, R. M. (1974). The theory of stochastic preference and brand switching. *Journal of Marketing Research, 11*, 1–20.

Bavetta, S., & del Seta, M. (2001). Constraints and the measurement of freedom of choice. *Theory and Decision, 50*, 213–238.

Bossert, W., Pattanaik, P., & Xu, Y. (1994). Ranking opportunity sets: An axiomatic approach. *Journal of Economic Theory, 63*, 326–345.

Edwards, J. (1834/1974). A careful and strict inquiry into the modern prevailing notions of that freedom of will which is supposed to be essential to moral agency, virtue and vice, reward and punishment, praise and blame. In Patrick. H. Alexander (Ed.), *The works of Jonathan Edwards* (Vol. 1, pp. 511–776). Avon: The Bath Press.

Falmagne, J.-C. (1978). A representation theorem for finite random scale systems. *Journal of Mathematical Psychology, 18*, 52–72.

García de la Sienra, A. (2010). La estructura lógica de la teoría de las finanzas [The logical structure of finance theory]. *EconoQuantum, 6*, 81–98.

Gravel, N. (1994). Can a ranking of opportunity sets attach intrinsic importance to freedom of choice? *American Economic Review, 84*, 454–458.

Hawking, S., & Mlodinow, L. (2001). *The grand design*. New York, NY: Bantam Books.

Kant, I. (1998). *Critique of pure reason*. Cambridge: Cambridge University Press.

Khinchin, A. I. (1957). *Mathematical foundations of information theory*. New York, NY: Dover Publications.

Klemisch-Ahlert, M. (1993). Freedom of choice: A comparison of different rankings of opportunity sets. *Social Choice and Welfare, 10*, 189–207.

Krantz, D. H., Luce, R. D., Suppes, P., & Tversky, A. (1971). *Foundations of measurement I. Additive and polynomial representations*. New York, NY: Academic Press.

Luce, R. D., & Krantz, D. H. (1971). Conditional expected utility. *Econometrica, 39*, 253–271.

Rawls, J. (1971). *A theory of justice*. Cambridge, MA: Harvard University Press.

Richter, M. K. (1971). Rational choice. In J. S. Chipman, L. Hurwicz, M. K. Richter, & H. F. Sonnenschein (Eds.), *Preferences, utilities, and demand* (pp. 29–58). New York, NY: Harcourt Brace Jovanovich.

Savage, L. J. (1954). *The foundations of statistics* (1st ed.). New York, NY: Wiley.

Savage, L. J. (1972). *The foundations of statistics* (2nd ed.). New York, NY: Dover Publications.

Searle, J. (2001). *Rationality in action*. Cambridge, MA: MIT Press.

Shannon, C. E. (1948). A mathematical theory of communication. *Bell System Technical Journal, 27*, 379–423 and 623–656.

Suárez, F. (1961). *Disputaciones metafísicas*. Madrid: Editorial Gredos.

Suppes, P. (1984). *Probabilistic metaphysics*. Oxford: Basil Blackwell.

Suppes, P. (1996). The nature and measurement of freedom. *Social Choice and Welfare, 13*, 183–200.

Suppes, P. (2001). Rationality, habits and freedom. In N. Dimitri, M. Basili, & I. Gilboa (Eds.), *Cognitive processes and economic behavior* (pp. 137–167). New York, NY: Routledge.

Suppes, P., Krantz, D. H., Luce, R. D., & Tversky, A. (1989). *Foundations of measurement II. Geometric, threshold, and probabilistic representations*. New York, NY: Academic Press.

Von Neumann, J., & Morgenstern, O. (1947). *Theory of games and economic behavior*. Princeton, MA: Princeton University Press.

Weber, M. (1947). *Max Weber: The theory of social and economic organization*. Glencoe, IL: The Free Press.

INTERVIEW

The world in axioms: an interview with Patrick Suppes

Catherine Herfeld

I met Patrick Suppes on 18 March 2014 in his office at Stanford's *Center for Study of Language and Information*. Until his passing away in November of that same year, he was still actively engaged in research at the *Suppes Brain Research Lab*, a laboratory that he had founded in the 1990s and where he investigated questions around language and human cognition. We had arranged the interview long before our meeting, and when he entered the center, it became clear how busy he still was: responsibilities from various sides before the interview; phone calls and signature requests in between the interview. He had already reached the age of 92, but seemed more energetic than many colleagues half a century younger. This energy was also what struck me during the interview. I had probably not met somebody as broadly literate and eloquently articulated as Suppes before. That itself might not mean much. And it confirmed in a way what I had repeatedly read and heard about him from his former colleagues and his admirers who had interacted with and had followed him throughout his career. But what means much, I think, is that I was able to confirm this observation when he had reached his 90s.

Patrick Suppes had received his B.S. in meteorology at the University of Chicago in 1943 and his Ph.D. in philosophy at Columbia University under the supervision of Ernest Nagel in 1950. In that same year, he was appointed assistant and subsequently associate professor of philosophy at Stanford University, where he first came into contact with Tarski's logic and set-theoretical models. In 1959, Suppes was appointed professor for philosophy as well as director of the *Institute for Mathematical* Studies in the Social Sciences at Stanford University. He had stayed at Stanford ever since, and he never really retired.

I conducted the interview for a book project entitled *Conversations on Rational Choice Theory*, which aims at bringing together the views of scholars who were and still are engaged with developing and applying various approaches of rational decision-making within and beyond economics. An interview with Suppes was a natural choice for such a project and for multiple reasons. One reason was that throughout his life, Suppes had been one of the strongest defenders of the axiomatic method in his work, a major ingredient of modern theories of rational choice. He had been deeply involved in working on the foundations of psychology and was one of the pioneers in using formal mathematical tools to approach human decision-making when they had been introduced in the 1950s and 1960s into the social and behavioral sciences. Beyond that, Suppes had worked on problems around the foundations of physics, on the theory of measurement, the measurement of utility and subjective probability in uncertain situations, and on learning theory. His research covered topics in philosophy of science, such as problems around causation. And he made pioneering contributions to computerized learning, the development and testing of general learning theory, and the semantics and syntax of natural language in philosophy of language. Given this wide range of contributions, Suppes, he was a polymath, and as such, he will always be remembered.

Catherine Herfeld: Professor Suppes, what do you take rational choice theory to be?

Patrick Suppes: Generally speaking, it is an axiomatic theory of choice. But I think that although it is as such a highly mathematical theory, we see the right continued development of it in recent years. It has become an ever-richer empirical subject, in terms of bringing in additional concepts.

C: What do you think it is that makes it a *theory* of rational choice? Is it the axiomatic representation of a given set of rationality principles?

S: Making a theory of rationality can be done axiomatically but does not have to. However, despite the development towards a more empirical theory, I ultimately think that the right way to do it is axiomatically, if one can. I think the axiomatic theory plays a particular role in isolating things, where it is said that it is hopeless to verbally theorize about without contradiction.

C: What makes rational choice theory to be a theory of *rational* choice?

S: I am very wary of the use of the word rational. I talk about choice theory. Delete rational!

C: When did you first encounter the axiomatic method?

S: I worked very closely with David Blackwell and Meyer Girshick. Herman Rubin and I studied their book *The Theory of Games and Statistical Decisions* very carefully. That was an influential book on theory of games and decisions in the 1950s and 1960s and it was really important for me.

C: When did you first encounter the axiomatic method?

I think I had two forces in my life at work that influenced my axiomatic view. One was working on the book by Blackwell and Girshick in particular. The other was Alfred Tarski, with whom I became acquainted in Berkeley during the time I studied game theory. I met Tarski, but that was also because J.C.C. McKenzie was here at Stanford. He must have been on the order of 10 or 12 years older than me. And he knew Tarski from back in the 1930s and so, on account of him, I met Tarski. We had very close interaction with Berkeley, with a lot of the Berkeley students, and they had a completely axiomatic view of the world that was dominant, foundational at that time.

C: You mention in your autobiography that you were organizing an informal seminar already during your graduate studies in philosophy at Columbia University where you discussed the *Theory of Games and Economic Decisions* by John von Neumann and Oskar Morgenstern. What had raised this early interest in game theory before you came to Stanford University?

S: Yes, in 1947–1948 we read the theory of games with some graduate students. My advisor in philosophy was Ernest Nagel. My history is complicated because of interruptions due to the war. My interests had been originally in physics, and so I came to philosophy only after the war on the Servicemen's Readjustment Act, i.e., the G.I. Bill of rights. I continued to work while the government supported me as a graduate student in philosophy. At Ernest's encouragement, I took both graduate courses in physics and mathematics, and from both of the directions, particularly the mathematics, as far as axiomatics goes, there was somebody who was quite prominent, Samuel Eilenberg. He was a Polish mathematician, a topologist, who exemplified a very abstract view. He gave beautiful lectures on group theory, which were very abstract, though, much to the disgust of the physicists, who expected from group theory something more practical. That was in 1947 and 1948.

C: Back then, the axiomatic method was important mostly in mathematics and physics. What did you, as a philosopher, expect from the axiomatic method at that time?

S: I became interested in it during a time when contemporary mathematics was just making a transition to a more or less full adoption of a set-theoretical axiomatic viewpoint about mathematics and so there is a lot conceptual lens throwing in and old-fashioned analysts did not like it. When I came to Stanford for example in 1950, we had some superb European analysts who were refugees. They were trained mathematicians of an older generation. They had been raised on analysis, according to which there was only one real system for them. They did not think of it axiomatically. Real and complex analysis, this was the truth for them. And they were remarkable. They did beautiful work, but without an emphasis on axiomatics. The point is that it was complicated. At the same time, there was this corresponding movement in the United States that was really emphasized by a number of people, and I got early support on account of it, to support people with mathematical background to work in the social and behavioral sciences. And, for various reasons, a lot of our work was axiomatic in character.

C: What were the reasons for taking this focus?

S: That is a good question. This was in the late 1940s and early 1950s. I think it reflected the fact that, preceding that, there had been this big turn to axiomatic methods in mathematics itself. If you had looked at mathematics in America before or during the war in, say 1937, this would not have been that way. Mathematics itself was not done so axiomatically. So the transition had been happening in mathematics. It was accelerated by people like Eilenberg and other scholars at Columbia, but particularly Eilenberg. He was a great influence there. And that sort of spilled. That's surely some off the cuff insights into this history that are probably correct. Ken Arrow was involved in this early history before I was.

C: The axiomatic method eventually became adopted in psychology and the social sciences. This is interesting because initially it did not naturally lend itself to address many of the core problems in those disciplines.

S: That is true. A lot of people did not like it. But then Ken Arrow's dissertation had some examples of showing the use of the axiomatic method in economics, showing negatively to how certain things are impossible. I think similar things happened in the theory of preference, maybe related to what Arrow did but now focused on the individual. And there was a lot of dispute about subjective probability and about utility theory. Such disputes – similar to much earlier disputes like Zermelo-Fraenkel set theory – are responses to what seemed to be contradictions. In other words, the use of axiomatics is inspired by contradictions.

The axiomatic method has this old tradition. It was probably really first introduced in an important mathematical way by the ancient Greeks. The ancient Greeks were responding to the very first problem. More precisely, there were two problems together, namely that the square root of 2 and pi are rational numbers. And there was huge dispute about this in the fourth or fifth century B.C. It is really in Greek mathematics where the axiomatic method did begin. It was so unbelievably sophisticated already then. There was nothing corresponding to this mathematical sophistication of the Greeks. Remember the problem was to prove consistency, so you had already both the axioms and the problem of consistency.

In the case of set theory, it goes back to Zermelo-Fraenkel set theory. In 1900, David Hilbert, at the international congress of mathematics, gave a list of famous open problems. Problem number one was to prove the continuum hypothesis. And of course he believed it could be proved. After the earlier work from Ernst Zermelo and Abraham Fraenkel, including Kurt Gödel's work, the most striking piece of work was Paul Cohen's proof of the independence of the axiom of choice from Zermelo-Fraenkel set theory. What that showed was, in some sense, the limitations of our thinking about what should be the foundations of mathematics. It showed that it is not just routine but rather that once we have done that, then there are real problems with how to think about what is the total foundation.

C: Together with Kurt Gödel's two incompleteness theorems and also John von Neumann's confrontation with the limitations of axiomatization in mathematics, this history did not necessarily make the axiomatic method attractive. Why did scholars begin to use the axiomatic method extensively in the social sciences?

S: Well, you have to remember something else. We had these results but historically, scholars had made this huge effort in others parts of science, but especially mathematics, to provide an axiomatic foundation. This urge, generated way back with the Greeks, came from the belief that the proper way to do things in mathematics and the sciences was in that way. Ptolemy's astronomy, written in about 100 AD is in some sense a more rigorous book about astronomy, including observations, than a lot of work that came much later by astronomers in the twentieth-century.

Ptolemy had written in this very rigorous, Euclidean fashion. And you see they also have a problem, like the continuum hypothesis. Ptolemy's astronomy was based upon the hypothesis, starting with Eudoxos, that all the orbits are circular, or compositions of circles. They discovered quite early that simple circles would not work and that you needed the composition of circles. Yet, these circles had a very strong restriction as part of their classical theory of axiomatic foundations of astronomy. The angular velocity must be constant, of the rotation of the Earth. They found already in Ptolemy's time that this would not work, unless you had many more convolutions of circles, which they did not want. So they would add either epicycles or epicenters. An epicycle is where you have an orbit and now you introduce a small [perturbation of an] orbit on the circumference. An epicenter is where you dislocate the center, which was a very big move, from being at the center of the Earth. So epicenter was to move the center off in order to fit the trajectory of a particular planet.

Now of course it was Apoloneus who proved the equivalence of these two mathematically, which is quite surprising. They have many different mathematical descriptions. Any orbit that had an epicenter representation had also an epicycle and conversely. So already there you see that it was considered very important to understand, starting from a very clear axiomatic basis, how the universe was working. And the impulse to that came out of this Greek tradition. It did not exist in Babylonia. The Babylonians were very good at computing, but at least all the stone tablets that we have read so far do not show anything comparable at all to Greek thought in this axiomatic way.

I think this history is very important to understand this history of axiomatics. And what is interesting is that it was not just pure mathematics. The application of mathematics to the motion of the heavens was *the* most successful empirical example in the ancient world. There were other good examples; some work in mechanics by people like for example Archimedes. But that was above all the most striking example.

C: Was the use of the axiomatic method primarily an attempt to make the social sciences more scientific in the 1950s?

S: Sure, absolutely. But I think that there was another impulse, which had been the same one that dominated Greek early thought, namely to address these paradoxes that we were talking about. Some of those paradoxes have a long history, like for example the gambler's fallacy. So, there has also been a long history regarding the work on decision-making and betting. And particularly here, axiomatization was an attempt to get rid of those paradoxes. One basic impulse is, when you have a paradox that seems to give you a contradiction in your intuitive way of thinking, try to axiomatize what you think the true theory is. Because a true theory that is consistent cannot have paradoxes.

C: Axiomatization seems to have had a different effect in the behavioral and social sciences. Take the kind of paradoxes that Leonard Savage encountered in the early 1950's with the axioms of his subjective expected utility theory or the Allais paradox. Those examples seem to be different from those you have in mind because they were provoked from the empirical weakness of those axioms. Savage himself failed to conform to his axioms.

S: And he then felt the axioms needed modification.

C: Those paradoxes did not arise from internal inconsistency of the system but rather from failing to conform to empirical evidence. One response of Savage to

Maurice Allais was that indeed those axioms were not useful for empirical, but only for normative purposes.

S: Well of course that is a different kind of response. And Savage wrote his book in 1954. That was in the early days. The literature became huge on this, particularly in economics and in psychology. Even today, there is a new discussion. And one attempt of a new discussion was to try to eliminate problems by giving an appropriate axiomatic foundation. In many of the cases, consistency is much more a problem in the minds of mathematicians than it is of economists. But although Savage just reinterpreted his theory, there was still some concern to show that theories were consistent.

C: Indeed. Arrow's proof of inconsistency was, according to Arrow himself, a reason for why his dissertation was very much regarded as something profound.

S: I think people also realized that there was a huge amount of cluttered normative thinking. And one of the ways to show that this does not all fit together well is to show that they are inconsistent, and then the question is what kind of positive consistent theory can you construct, and the natural way of doing that is to think axiomatically. That is, the axiomatic method is a natural response to the existence of inconsistencies in intuitive thinking. I think that is an important idea. Do you agree with that or not?

C: One would probably agree with that if committed to a particular image of science

S: This is theoretical thinking about science. Maybe this thinking can be also empirical because empirical data are also used to show that classical theories do not work.

C: What is the usefulness of mathematics in science apart from guaranteeing the consistency of the theories?

S: Mathematics, and also statistics, is most useful when it can also be used for predictive purposes. The history of axiomatics in mathematics turned out to be much more convoluted than it had been thought. The results of Gödel and Cohen and other people show that you cannot prove consistency unless using a theory that is more powerful. You could not prove ordinary mathematics, let's say classical analysis, as being consistent without using a theory that was still more powerful, and whose proof of consistency was even harder than the theory you're using it to prove. But you could not prove with a system of the same strength that it was consistent. That's a great result.

Arrow's impossibility theorem is a much more specialized theorem than those big time theorems in mathematics as a whole. But, it is also an important result.

C: What do you consider the empirical usefulness of such a theoretical undertaking?

S: It takes some of the wind out of the sails of overblown theories, and you cut theory back to having a more empirical character. For example, if you want to be very finitistic, you can prove consistency. Something you can do is to discuss the consistency of arithmetic, if you consider no number larger than some fixed natural number. There was a discussion about these aspects, about finitistic theories of utility, in the 1950's. The problem with Savage's book of 1954 was that he used infinite sets of states, etc. which clashes with the real world. It was written in a specific way, in a kind of classical mathematical style. One kind of response was that we can be finitistic about this. Now, I think economics has not stayed that way in general at all. In fact it is very unusual to have highly constructive finitistic theories in economics. They have gone back to depending mainly on classical analysis.

C: Recently economists have made new attempts to improve economic theories of behavior by taking psychological and neuroscientific results more seriously.

S: Sure, and that's the direction of complexity.

C: One hope might be that psychological theories could replace traditional axiomatic choice theories at some point.

S: Well I think the following point isn't always made explicit and it has its own weaknesses, but if you make everything sufficiently finitistic, then, in principle, you can just give that. Axiomatics can be given in a kind of clear but uninteresting way. So you have a finite set of axioms; the models are all finite. But, some of those models will lead to very complicated sets of axioms. And of course what people want is something that is more reduced than that. So what may happen, if you abandon trying to give relatively simple axiomatic theories, is that the theory now no longer has a clear formulation. Much of economics is still that way. All you have to do is turn on the TV to see and to listen to amateur economics discussed endlessly. And so what happens is that you no longer have a budding science; you have something much weaker.

C: Does this not depend on how axioms are justified? Your own work in psychology for example is highly formal in parts, yet it was significantly inspired by your empirical work.

S: Yes! Because my thrust was to get at what really the basic assumptions are in each case, in order to clarify what follows from them. Many of the people in psychology who wrote the theories didn't know any mathematics or very little.

C: Did economists just get it wrong with their axiom systems so far? Should they have taken other axioms that are more empirically inspired?

S: Remember you have something going on in economics that isn't mentioned enough on this side of discussion, and that is econometrics. So there was a strong statistical econometric tradition going back into the nineteenth-century, at least. And there was not a strong interaction between these two. I do not think that econometrics is mentioned once in Savage's book, for example.

In the neoclassical tradition of economics, there are so many theoretical papers that don't come even close to data of any kind. And that's very important, because I think that the big difference between economists and psychologists is that while economists are better theoreticians, psychologists are much better at having found good data to try to support theories. In Kenneth Arrow's thesis, for example, there is almost no flow of experiments that directly follow from that work. What flows from it is a body of theoretical work.

C: At which level could data enter the picture in such a theoretical framework?

S: What actually happened in physics is a good example. Newton's work was not purely theoretical. Rather, there was a continual interaction between theoretical and empirical work, i.e. between the data and the correct estimation of the parameters in the theory. That is the glory of celestial mechanics; in the eighteenth-century, particularly at the end of the 17th, it was recognized that you had this very powerful interaction between theory and data. It wasn't even about experiments because what they used was astronomical data. But, sure that doesn't really occur too often.

C: Some economists tried when they considered classical mechanics as their role model for a very long time and considered utility theory as a useful starting point for economic theorizing as it approximated human behavior in the market sphere.

S: But name an economist who was serious about that. They weren't serious about it. That's one thing that's very hard work.

C: William Stanley Jevons or Vilfredo Pareto?

S: Well Jevons and Pareto were too late. I'm talking about the earlier period. Newton's famous papers on this were written at the end of the seventeenth-century, and they had a big impact on scientific work in the eighteenth-century.

C: Economics is a much younger science than physics. What some economists tried was looking at the successful theories in physics and then formulating an analogous theoretical framework for economics. They believed that they might be able to arrive at a theory that could be based on a small set of behavioral laws that could ultimately be formulated in mathematical terms.

S: I think it is nonsense. It is really romantic nonsense.

C: Formulating a general theory of human behavior and social interaction seems to be just a huge challenge ...

S: It is the same challenge in physics. I remember a famous lecture I heard in the late 1940s or early 1950s by a prominent mathematical physicist. He said: we owe our students an apology. We have taught them as if physics is really simple, when in fact, we as physicists can only solve the simplest cases completely. So I like to say that celestial mechanics is really a great science, for $n = 1$ it's fine, for $n = 2$ you can do very well, but go to $n = 3$ particles, and you're stuck. The behavior you cannot give a complete account of. And that isn't very far into it. And if you go to relativistic mechanics, classical mechanics now formulated for relativistic purposes, $n = 2$ is not solvable in closed form, so it's only $n = 1$. Quantum mechanics is completely weak in studying the interaction of atoms or particles or whatever it may be.

C: In your autobiography, you state that your knowledge of meteorology had stood you "in good stead throughout the years in refuting arguments that attempt to draw some sharp distinction between the precision and perfection of the physical sciences and the vagueness and imprecision of the social sciences. Meteorology is in theory a part of physics, but in practice more like economies, especially in the handling of a vast flow of nonexperimental data." (Suppes 1978) This sounds very

much like what Kenneth Arrow said, when talking about his disappointments with physics as an inexact science when he worked as a meteorologist. You were both disappointed by physics, because it turned out that physics is not the exact science that you thought it was. If neither physics nor economics have achieved to be exact sciences, what does that imply – conceptually and methodologically – for how those sciences should be practices?

S: Yes, Ken and I discuss that regularly, we were both meteorologists in World War II. My view that I've come to gradually late in life, is that science is mainly extremely fragmentary in character as opposed to the idea of it being a well-organized thorough body of knowledge that explains to us mainly how the universe works. Like experience, it is very fragmentary. The cases can be studied thoroughly are extremely limited.

C: Some people might argue that this would go against one of the most important motivations for axiomatics.

S: No, not at all. At least what you've got you can study axiomatically. What you haven't got, you can't study at all. In that sense, axiomatics help clarify. Only if you start with a very clear basis you can come to see that the situation is in fact hopeless. If you don't have a strong firm basis, people can think mistakenly. If we think of the right function here, we're going to be able to get our way through this. Whereas starting from a clear axiomatic basis, to prove incompleteness or insolubility, or the impossibility of a closed form solution to a differential equation, is a great triumph of the human intellect to understand that the world is complicated. And only if you had a good foundation do you believe those proofs being correct. I mean that's probably one of the best examples that very familiar differential equations, both ordinary and partial, do not have closed form solutions.

C: That is interesting, because for example your work on the foundations of measurement was an attempt of trying to lay the foundations of measurement for all the sciences.

S: My own view changed; my earlier views, when I was younger, were wrong. When one is younger, one is too naïve. I was, and most people are, too naïve about the possibility of having genuine wide-ranging semi-complete solutions to things. That is much too optimistic. And it has taken a long time to realize the fact that what we can do with mathematics about natural phenomena is much more limited than was originally thought. Meteorology is a good help to see that. Everybody talks about the weather but nobody can thoroughly understand it scientifically in terms of what you would like to have. You would like being able to predict the weather two weeks from now. That is an insight that has come late to me.

C: In your work in the 1950's with Donald Davidson and Sidney Siegel you did experiments where you showed that the results of expected utility theory were not that satisfying.

S: We already showed that in these finitistic cases, it didn't work out the way you liked.

C: Did this already lead you to doubts about a science of rationality?

S: Absolutely. This was in the special case for rationality. But now I am talking about a wider generalization of mine, that this intuitive science in general is fragmentary in character. Almost no problem of any complexity can be solved completely in science. And we have illusions of grandeur as to what we can do theoretically.

C: Was this early work driven by the general idea that we can find the general axioms of the social sciences?

S: It was a mistake to think we're going to do that, finding general axioms of the social sciences. The discussions of Savage and others turned out to be dominated by a very naïve view about human behavior. And I think some of the things that I probably wrote then, I would now consider naïve, even though I was already on the side of the position that it is hard to solve things, hard to find cases where utility theory really works.

C: One could argue also that this kind of work has nevertheless certain usefulness. First, utility theory had some specific features that were useful at least for modeling purposes. Second, its usefulness might also depend on the problem at hand, which varies across disciplines. The theory might suit for one purpose better than for another.

S: Well measurement was one thing. I think theoretically I would consider my work on stochastic learning models as more important in psychology. But certainly measurement has been important in psychology. It had its important place in economics as part of a general discussion. I am in my reflective later years now and I can say that. But already back then, I think Duncan Luce pushed us more in the direction of mathematics and the foundations of measurement than I thought was a good idea. I can remember our discussion about those issues and about how they should be handled. I thought we should deal more with finitistic examples, the statistics of real measurement and I can remember Dave Krantz saying that the trouble would be that it would going to be too hard to do thoroughly. My own criticism of the foundations of measurement was that too much time was spent on what I would consider as being not very interesting, reasonably elementary, mathematics. It would have been much better to have given a much more thorough treatment of finite models with error, and to have analyzed the theory of error, the statistics of error very thoroughly because this was something psychologists themselves did not and don't know and understand too well. Yet, we didn't lead the way we should've, that's my personal view. Upon reflection, this is my criticism of that work in which I partly joined in and as such it is criticism of myself.

C: What did you think of axiomatic work in economics such as Gerard Debreu's *Theory of Value*?

S: I have the same criticism of Debreu, and I knew him quite well. He never really applied a theory in detail to any complicated data.

C: Why do you think economists have not been as much concerned with applying their theories to complicated data as they were with developing complicated theories?

S: I think that this is an interesting historical question. Why have there been these two rather separate traditions in economics? What is interesting about it is that the people who have been interested in data are often quite sophisticated mathematically, because they have a background in mathematical statistics. That's good but it's a different background. The development of the theory of mathematical statistics took place in the 1940s and 1950s. Many of those people, Kenneth Arrow for example with lots of mathematical background, were also working in economics, I mean, for example, the whole theory of IID random variables, and the asymptotic theory of that, which has its own application, it's also beautiful mathematically, but that was really something very different than, say, neoclassical theory.

For us, an important book such as for example J.L. Doob's *Stochastic Processes* was only published in the 1950's. One of the things we wanted to understand was the clarification of probability, and we were not so much concerned with statistics. Initially, the Russians had best done this. Take Andrei Kolomogorov's famous work in German, which had been published earlier in Russian, was only 1933. We were very late, and the Russians were determined to show that probability theory should be a standard mathematical theory. So there's no question, you see, that the Russians were numero uno in the first half of the twentieth-century in probability theory. There were good people elsewhere, but the Russians dominated the results. And what they were showing, that there was a strong mathematical theory required to solve standard conceptual problems in probability theory.

Too many people ignore the Russians. The Russian tradition was not really statistical, but it was probability all the way down. They were late to really digging fully into modern statistical procedure, with the random variable set up, and data, etc. that is, that whole modern set up of mathematical statistics. And yet they proved the largest body of important theorems. The largest body was clearly proved by the Russians, starting with Alexandre Lyapunov and that is all written down in Andrey's Kolmogorov's work. And their work is also an interesting example of axiomatic theory. Kolmogorov is very clear about being axiomatic. He says it's like Hilbert's axioms. He was wrong there because he doesn't start with qualitative axioms and derive a quantitative representation, but clearly it is axiomatically written, and he's very clear about writing it that way. And that was a clarifying thing already in 1933, which is pretty early in this story, that's like roughly 23 years before Kenneth Arrow's dissertation was published. It took two decades. And that was a very important influence in probability theory.

I mention probability theory for an important reason because it has been so important in the social and behavioral sciences as a mathematical apparatus. But the firm foundations of probability theory don't date much before 1933. Laplace had done interesting work and Abraham De Moivre but really getting the foundations straight, axiomatically, came quite late, which is an interesting story in itself.

C: In economics, J.M. Keynes wrote his treatise on probability …

S: Yes, but it is terrible. It's a mess. It's particularly a mess, given when it was written and given that the Russian had done before. And on the scientific side, Keynes's book on probability never had a big impact, and rightly so.

C: What makes an axiomatic theory a good theory?

S: I think Isaac Newton's work was good. Newton really clarified in some deep way how to think about the foundations of mechanics, which was not so clearly done before. That doesn't mean there aren't predecessors. But Newton was the one who really crystallized it. And what's important about this is that he wasn't just crystallizing the foundations, but he was doing something important with it, namely to develop an axiomatic theory of gravitational interaction, that is, the most pervasive and important and mystifying approach of gravity. We still don't quite know how we want to explain gravity, but we certainly know that gravity is there. And Newton said he had no place for hypotheses. He clarified, without explaining it in some philosophical way, what gravity is. He clarified what the laws are, the primary law, of attraction. And that was a very important clarification. Descartes' theory of gravitation, for example, was hopeless. It was a field theory, so there wouldn't be action at a distance, but of course it was physically wrong and it was shown decisively so by Newton and others. Two generations after Newton they were still using Descartes in the introductory course of physics at Cambridge University. So the world moves slowly.

C: Was the work of von Neumann and Morgenstern on formulating a theory of human *interaction* comparable in its significance for the social sciences?

S: Some people think that and I think actually, in the terms of the methodological effect it has had, there is some sense that John von Neumann's big treatise on the theory of games had a big impact, in introducing a way of thinking formally about multiperson interactions.

C: In your paper *General Remarks on the Study of Preference*, you argue that human behavior is hugely complex, which limits the empirical value of any simple and general psychological theory of decision-making. At the same time, you criticize the heavy focus in economics on optimization, which – one could argue – comes however with the benefit of being able to use mathematics to formulate economic problems in a precise manner. How do you think should the trade off between an empirically more adequate and useful theory of human behavior and a simple mathematical theory be made?

S: I think, of course, that the empirical side wins that battle. The world is not going to change in some drastic way to satisfy some simple theory of optimization. So, you're not going to change the world. Rather, you have to change your theory.

C: Scientists almost always have to idealize …

S: Not necessarily. Not when it's going to lead you in a lot of bad predictions. If my job in the world were to be an opponent – which it's not – of neoclassical economics, I'd rub their nose in the fact that they are not able to predict anything correctly. Everything is different from what they say it is. So why should we take seriously their ideas? And they would have to respond to that.

C: The subject of economics, namely the economy, seems to be very similar to the subject of the meteorologist, namely the weather. Would it be best to acknowledge that we cannot predict very well the weather two weeks in advance and consider rethinking the idea of having an axiomatic theory all together?

S: One of the things about economics today is that you need proofs of chaotic behavior, because the basic equations are chaotic. And that's not necessarily true of all the equations of neoclassical economics. The equations in those theories are not chaotic, and that's what's wrong with the example. You might ask what the problem is in understanding the elementary processes in the weather. How could the predictions be so bad? The answer is that the theory is chaotic. There's no hope of having extended predictions from it. That's the nature of chaotic systems. One typical feature is that they are so unbelievably sensitive to initial conditions. Another example from physics is turbulence. Turbulence gets generated in the process of things occurring that are themselves unpredictable. But none of that's discussed at all in economics.

Take for example something like modern finance. Modern finance is just full of unbelievably complex instruments. None of those instruments are discussed carefully in the theory in this broad neoclassical tradition.

C: There are some attempts in econophysics that try to push in this direction ...

S: Right, and that's a good idea. That is the direction to go.

C: Would this imply a shift in focus away from studying individual decision-making with the aid of simple experiments towards studying the behavior of a complex system?

S: I think there's the following correct moral idea of what you're saying. We don't really do experiments in meteorology that are very successful and useful. We think there have been experiments that are useful, but we don't feel the need for that, because it is evident that this doesn't compare to how to deal with the chaotic behavior of the systems that are approximately correct. But that is in fact the *real* problem.

C: Should economists then depart from an axiomatic representation of human behavior?

S: In meteorology, we start with continuous equations. But those equations describe behavior of continuous fluids that are, by assumption, considered continuous for mathematical approximation. For the purposes of the weather, they can be treated as such even though we all know they're not, in a mathematical sense, continuous. So whether economists should start with equations that describe the behavior of human agents is a question of what's going to work, not necessarily about how far to go in the reduction. The approximation of continuity in that assumption is not bad, if all you look at is the study of the flow of the saturation of water and the water vapor in the atmosphere. Studying it as a continuous process, that aspect of approximation is not where the problems are. It's not those approximations that are the source of the problem, almost surely. Rather, the source is that large-scale systems that are chaotic.

C: So how important do you consider the current work in psychology and behavioral economics?

S: Social psychologists, for example, don't even know what a chaotic system is, at least most of them.

Whether the claim that you can show that economic systems are chaotic is true of an economic system is a nice question. And it is a long way from the current mathematical investigations. It took quite sophisticated theoretical investigation to prove that the weather system is, to first approximation, chaotic. Economists should give it a try.

By the way, in this context I should remark that Edward Norton Lorenz should be regarded as the most famous meteorologist of the twentieth-century. He really proved these things most successfully. He was my fellow predictor in Guam of bombing of Tokyo, he and I prepared the predictions for the winds over 10,000 feet every day. 12 h on, 12 h off, in the last months of World War II. And the largest American air base by far, for bombing Tokyo, in Guam, Saipan, and another third island. Headquarters were in Guam, when I was in the weather central for the 20th air force. We bombed Tokyo every day. People don't realize, that we killed more people in Tokyo than we killed with the atomic bomb. Another year and we'd have destroyed Tokyo. Every day he and I had the responsibility to predict the weather, and particularly the upper air winds, the planes were coming in at 20,000 feet, what were going to be the dominant winds. If you predicted a B29 to come in on the wrong way, the winds were strong enough that the plane almost was stationary over Tokyo for too long, to be hit by anti-aircraft. You had to bring them in a way they got out of there fast. But that is only a side note.

C: Should mathematics be the central ingredient of economic theories?

S: Of course! Nobody is going to have a serious theory about anything that is complicated that does not use mathematics. They may think so, but they are just kidding themselves. And you have people who are deceived about that. They think that they can verbalize some really complicated phenomena successfully. We have had a bunch of experimental psychologists in history who felt that way. Well, I have to say that they are wrong!

C: Are you after truth?

S: Yes, I'm all for truth. It's just hard to achieve – its fragmentary.

Funding

This research was supported by the Humboldt Foundation, Germany.

Reference

Suppes, P. (1978). *Intellectual Autobiography, 1922–1978*. p. 2. Retrieved from https://suppes-corpus.stanford.edu/pdfs/Intellectual%20Autobio.pdf

Index

For Product Safety Concerns and Information please contact our EU
representative GPSR@taylorandfrancis.com Taylor & Francis Verlag GmbH,
Kaufingerstraße 24, 80331 München, Germany

Printed and bound by CPI Group (UK) Ltd, Croydon, CR0 4YY
01/05/2025
01858459-0008